THE WOODS
LAKEBOAT
EDMOND

Works by David Mamet
Published by Grove Press

American Buffalo

The Cherry Orchard
(adapted from Anton Chekhov)

Five Television Plays

Glengarry Glen Ross

Goldberg Street:
Short Plays and Monologues

Homicide

House of Games: A Screenplay

A Life in the Theatre

Reunion *and* Dark Pony

Sexual Perversity in Chicago *and*
The Duck Variations

The Shawl *and* Prairie du Chien

Speed-the-Plow

Things Change: A Screenplay
(with Shel Silverstein)

Three Children's Plays

Warm and Cold
(with Donald Sultan)

We're No Angels

The Woods, Lakeboat, Edmond

THE WOODS
LAKEBOAT
EDMOND

Three Plays by
DAVID MAMET

Grove Press
NEW YORK

Printed in the United States of America

Library of Congress Cataloging-in-Publication Data

Mamet, David.
  The woods; Lakeboat; and Edmond.

    I. Title. II. Title: Woods. III. Title: Lakeboat.
IV. Title: Edmond.
PS3563.A4345A6   1987   812'.54   86-33489
ISBN 0-8021-5109-4

Grove Press
841 Broadway
New York, NY 10003

98 99 00 01 10 9 8 7 6 5 4

Contents

THE WOODS

The Woods was first produced by the St. Nicholas Theater Company, Chicago, Illinois, November 11, 1977, with the following cast:

RUTH	Patti LuPone
NICK	Peter Weller

This production was directed by David Mamet; set by Michael Merritt; lighting by Robert Christen; graphic design by Lois Grimm; presented in arrangement with Ken Marsolais.

Scenes:

1. Dusk
2. Night
3. Morning

Characters:

RUTH
NICK

Setting:

The porch of a summer house, early September.

Scene 1

Dusk

Ruth *and* Nick *are sitting on the porch.*

Ruth: These seagulls they were up there, one of them was
   up there by himself.
   He didn't want the other ones.
   They came, he'd flap and get them off.
   He let this one guy stay up there a minute.

Nick: Tell me.

Ruth: They flew off.

   (Pause.)

Nick: We have a lot of them. And herons.

Ruth: You have herons?

Nick: Yes. I think. I haven't seen them in a while.
   We did when I was young.

Ruth: Do they stay in the Winter, too?

Nick: No.

Ruth *(to self):* No.
   We'll need more blankets soon.

13

NICK: Were you cold last night?

RUTH: I think you were dreaming. Yes. A little.
    You took all the blankets. Were you dreaming?

NICK: Yes.

RUTH: I thought so. I hunched over next to you.
    I held you.
    Could you feel that?

NICK: Yes.

RUTH: I went down for a walk.

NICK: Where?

RUTH: Down by the Lake. All around.
    I sat down and I listened, you know?
    To the laps.
    Time passed.

   (Pause.)

    I threw these stones.
    I picked this stick up and I drew with it.

NICK: What did you draw?

RUTH: All sorts of things.

NICK: What?

RUTH: Patterns.

   (Pause.)

    The fish jumped. Everything smelled like iodine.

NICK: Mmmm.

RUTH: You could live up here. Why not?

(Pause.)

People could.
You could live right out in the country.
I slept so good yesterday.
All the crickets. You know?
With the rhythm.
You wait.
And you hear it.
Chirp.
Chirp chirp.
Not "chirping."

(Pause.)

Not *"chirping,"* really.
Birds chirp.
Birds chirp, don't they, Nick?
Birds?

NICK: Crickets, too, I think.

RUTH: Yes?

NICK *(to self):* "I heard crickets chirp."
"The crickets chirped."
(Aloud.) Yes.

RUTH: I thought so. What do frogs do?

NICK: They croak.

(Pause.)

RUTH: I listened. All night long. They get soft at dawn.
Maybe they go to sleep.

Maybe the sun makes the air different and they become harder to hear. I don't know.

(*Pause.*)

Who knows what's happening?
Down by the Lake there is a rotten boat.
A big green rowboat.
It might be from here to here.
It's rotten and the back is gone, but I'll bet it was
pretty big.
I sat in it.
Inside the front was pointed up. It smelled real dry.
I mooshed around and this is how it sounded on the
sand.
Swssshh. Chhhrssssh. Swwwssshhhh.
Very dry.
You know. I think I would of liked to go to sea.
Girls couldn't go to sea.
As cabin boys or something . . .

NICK: They had woman pirates.

RUTH: They were outlaws. Men would not let women go
to sea.

NICK: The Vikings.

RUTH: They let women go?

NICK: Sure.

RUTH: No. No. I don't think so.

NICK: No?

RUTH: Uh-uh. I heard of Vikings. Viking Women.
They would stay home and make clothes.

They used to bash the babies' heads in.
All the little girls.
They'd kill them. Did you know that, Nicky?

NICK: Yes.

RUTH: At birth?

NICK: Yes.

(Pause.)

RUTH: You heard that?

NICK: Yes. I read it.

(Pause.)

RUTH: Not all of them.
A lot of them.
The Vikings.

(Pause.)

Poor babes.
What do you think of that?

NICK: Give me a kiss. *(She goes to him. They kiss.)*

RUTH: I like it here.

(Pause.)

Can you smell the iodine?

NICK: Yes.

RUTH: Ozone. Can you smell it? Can you smell ozone?

NICK: Now?

RUTH: No. I mean, does ozone smell?
    The thing itself?

NICK: I think so.

   (Pause.)

RUTH: They told us after the storms the ozone came from
    electricity.

NICK *(to self):* . . . electrical discharges.

RUTH: But now we have Ozone Alerts, they tell you it's no
    good for you.
    Who *knows* what's good for you?
    The Vikings had these lovely Northern Women and
    they used to bash their heads in.

   (Pause.)

   Oh, well.
   Oh, well.
   Who *knows* what's good for them?

   (Pause.)

   If this was mine, I'd come here all the time.
   I think it's wild here, Nick.
   I saw a raccoon.

NICK: When?

RUTH: Last night. On my walk.

NICK: You should have woke me up.

RUTH: You were asleep.

NICK: I would have gone with you.

RUTH: No. You were dreaming. And then when I saw it I was far from here. I heard a noise, I turned around, and there was this raccoon.

NICK: Where?

RUTH: Over there. I saw his eyes. He ran off.

NICK: They get in the garbage.

RUTH: No. I know. They eat it. When I saw it, I did not know what it was. Then it ran off.

(Pause.)

NICK: We had them up here all the time.

RUTH: When you were young.

NICK: We'd catch them in a milk container.

RUTH: Are they vicious?

NICK: Very.

RUTH: Yes. I thought so.

NICK: And you couldn't keep them 'cause they'd gnaw their way out.

RUTH: I was thinking . . . wait. Wait! They ate wood? The raccoons?

NICK: No. You know. They'd chew it.

RUTH: To get *out.*

NICK: Yes.

(Pause.)

RUTH: Yes. I was thinking.

NICK: Tell me.

RUTH: Things that people like.
I thought the things that people like—I should have woke you up 'cause I was thinking on my walk—I thought our *appetites* are just the body's way to tell us things that we may need.

(Pause.)

NICK *(looking at Lake):* Fishes.

RUTH: Where are they?

NICK: Down there.

(Pause.)

RUTH: What do you think? Our appetites.

NICK: Say it again.

RUTH: The liking that we have for things—desire—is just our body's way to tell us things.

(Pause.)

When we see someone—some woman on the beach—we say that she is beautiful.

(Pause.)

That's because perhaps of what is in her.
Small breasts. *(Pause.)* Maybe large.

The way she holds her back.
We see her and we know if we would breed with her,
the things that would come out of it improve the race.
What do you think about that? Appetites.

NICK: What about food?

(Pause.)

RUTH: What about it?

NICK: Tastes we have for it.

RUTH *(pause):* Tastes.

NICK: Yes.

RUTH: The tastes we have for it.

NICK: Yes.

RUTH: Food.

(Pause.)

Are you hungry?

NICK: No.

(Pause.)

RUTH: It must be the same.
Our body says we need these things.
They all come from the ground.
The vegetables.

(Pause.)

Minerals.
All pills and ointments.
Everything comes from the ground, in some way or
another.
Then we eat it.
Medicine . . . I've thought about this . . .
What they give us are just things that come out of the
ground.
Or that we make. If they are concentrated, or we alter
them, so we can swallow them.
All things come from the ground.

(Pause.)

And the way that they found out was folks would eat
them.
We would keep the good and we would pass the bad
things off.
I saw the fish grab insects right out of the air.
It all has properties. It all is only things the way they
are.

(Pause.)

That is all there ever was.

(Pause.)

What they are and what they do.
And that is beauty.

(Pause.)

NICK: What about cigarettes?

(Pause.)

RUTH: Cigarettes?

NICK: Yes.

RUTH: They are bad for you.

NICK: I know.

RUTH: Why do we smoke them?

NICK: Yes.

RUTH *(sigh):* We fall away from ourselves. We grow fat.
We fall away. The women, too. And men. We pick the
people that we know are bad for us. We do that all the
time.

NICK: We do. *(Pause.)* Why?

RUTH: I don't know. Nothing lasts. *(Pause.)* This is what I
thought down on the rowboat. It had rotted.
It had gone back to the Earth. We all go.
That is why the Earth is good for us.
When we look for things that don't go back, we be-
come sick.

(Pause.)

That is when we hurt each other.
I thought about you and me.

NICK: You did.

RUTH: Down on the rowboat, yes.

NICK: What did you think, Ruth?

RUTH: Coming up here. How you asked me.
    So little counts. Nick.
    Just the things we do.

    (Pause.)

    To each other. The right things.

    (Pause.)

    That's what I think. *(Pause.)*
    The frog *croaks?*

NICK: Come here.

RUTH: Does it?

NICK: Yes. Come here. *(She does so. They kiss.)*

RUTH: Are you happy now?

NICK: Yes.

RUTH: And she said they had a bear here.

NICK: Who said that?

RUTH: The woman.

NICK: When?

RUTH: Her mother saw one. Long ago.

NICK: *Here?*

RUTH: Right here.

NICK: When?

RUTH: When she was young.

NICK: A wild bear.

RUTH: Yes. She told me they had built the house upon its
cave, and it came back.
It used to keep on coming here.
And then it went away, and this is when she saw it, it
came back—her mother said—when it was going to
die. Just like in Russia.

(Pause.)

To get beneath the house.

NICK: When was this?

RUTH: Long ago.

NICK: A wild bear.

RUTH: Yes. A long, long time ago.

NICK: He'd be long dead now.

RUTH: *Long* dead.

NICK: They still have them up *there.*

RUTH: Where?

NICK: In Canada.

RUTH: Bears.

NICK: Not around here.

RUTH: No.

NICK: Up where it's wild.

RUTH: They have a lot of land.

NICK: Down, maybe, in the *cane*brakes.

RUTH: I don't think so. Most of them are gone.
But we can think about them.

(*Pause.*)

NICK: My father saw a bear once.

RUTH: He did. Where?

NICK: In the Black Forest.

RUTH: In the War?

NICK: Yes.

RUTH: Tell me.

NICK: Look. Look. Oh, my God.

RUTH: What?

(*Pause.*)

NICK (*pointing*): The beaver.

RUTH: Where?

(*Pause.*)

Where?

NICK: I'm pointing at it.

RUTH: I can't see it.

NICK: There. Look. There.

(*Pause.*)

See?

RUTH: Yes.

NICK: Do you see?

RUTH: Yes.

NICK: No. You don't see where I'm pointing.

RUTH: Yes. I do.

NICK: You do?

RUTH: Yes.

(Pause.)

NICK: What?

RUTH: It's a log.

NICK: What is?

RUTH: The beaver.

(Pause.)

NICK: The beaver is?

RUTH: Yes.

NICK: No. You don't see where I'm pointing.

RUTH: I don't think that we have beavers here.

NICK: You don't see where I'm pointing.

RUTH: Yes. I do.

NICK: There? Near the raft?

RUTH: Yes. It's a log.

(Pause.)

NICK: It's a *log?*

RUTH: I don't think we have beavers here.

(Pause.)

NICK: But I swear I saw it swimming.

RUTH: Sometimes something floats along it looks just like
    it's swimming.

(Pause.)

There's forces in the water.

(Pause.)

I know.
I used to fish for things when I was little.

NICK: You did?

RUTH: Yes. I did.

NICK: For what?

RUTH: These fish.
    These lovely fish.

NICK: What were they?

RUTH: I don't know. I think that they were perch. They
    tasted delicate. I used to clean them. I would get the
    smell upon my hands. When I was little.
    It smelled like I put my hands inside myself.
    I used to like to clean the fish.

One time I sat down on the dock I lost this bracelet
that my Grandmother gave me.
It floated down.

NICK: In summer?

RUTH: Yes. In Fall. I had the bracelet. I was on the dock.
(Pause.) I should not have been there.

(Pause.)

It fell.
It floated down. I dropped it.

(Pause.)

I can still see it.
Floating down.
It went so slowly.

(Pause.)

It was a necklace and I wore it as a bracelet.
Wrapped around.
My Grandmother's.

(Pause.)

NICK: Nothing lasts forever.

RUTH: We could do that.

NICK: What, Ruth?

RUTH: Wear things.

NICK: What?

RUTH: We could wear anything. Rings, bracelets.
Long, slim necklaces.
Gold necklaces.
We'd wear them on our wrists.

(Pause.)

Wrapped around.
To show that we are lovers.

(Pause.)

There are so many things that we could do.
I'm glad we came here.

(Pause.)

Do you know why I love it here?

(Pause.)

NICK: Why?

RUTH: Because it's clean.

NICK: We used to come here all the time.

RUTH: The Winter, too?

NICK: We'd drive up. In the Winter. Summers.

RUTH: You could come up any time you put up insulation.

NICK: Yes.

RUTH: And build the fires.

NICK: We came up here.

(Pause.)

RUTH: Did you?

NICK: Many times.

RUTH: Or maybe just the fireplace, you chinked it up.

NICK: We used to see these men. At stoplights.
Way before the Superhighways.

RUTH *(to self):* That was a long time ago.

NICK: They'd walk between the cars at stoplights
. . . selling flowers to the men.

RUTH: Huh!

NICK: Sometimes they had boards with little animals.

RUTH: No.

NICK: Yes.

RUTH: And they would sell them?

NICK: Yes.

RUTH: What happened to those men?

NICK: I don't know. *(Pause.)*
Or paper boys, they used to walk between the rows.
They'd cry, "All Late."

RUTH: "All Late."

NICK: Yes.

(Pause.)

RUTH: What did they mean?

NICK: The papers were all late.

RUTH: The papers were late.

NICK: Yes.

RUTH: The papers were late.

NICK: Yes.

(*Pause.*)

RUTH: They had a late edition.

NICK: Yes. Or sometimes they would have balloons.

RUTH: The paper boys?

NICK: No.

RUTH: No, I didn't think so.

NICK: They would sell balloons.
    Then you would go home.

RUTH: I would love it up here in the Winter.
    (*To self:*) Buying toys or flowers for their family.

NICK: Mmm.

RUTH: We could sit and watch the snow and make a fire.
    We could get a clock. We'd cuddle up inside our quilts
    and watch the fire.

NICK: We came up here in Winter one time.
    Many times.

RUTH: You did?

NICK: A few times.

RUTH: Tell me.

NICK: It was cold.

RUTH: I know. I bet it was.

NICK: We used to sit around, we'd make a fire.
  Sometimes he'd tell us stories of the Indians, or from
  the War.

  (Pause.)

RUTH: . . . sitting in the cold and he told stories from the
  War.
  I bet that you felt safe.

NICK: We did.

  (Pause.)

  And content.

RUTH: Because all things had stopped.

NICK: What?

RUTH: They had all stopped.
  You were up here where you wished to be. *(Pause.)*
  Mmm.

NICK: He used to sit out here all afternoon and work.

  (Pause.)

  In the Summertime.
  He'd weight the papers down with rocks.
  He'd sit and work all afternoon.

RUTH: You're like that, Nicky.

NICK: I am?

RUTH: I can watch you.

NICK: . . . in his shirtsleeves.

RUTH: . . . yes.
  Because you are serene.

  (Pause.)

  I know what you are.

  (Pause.)

  I know.

  (Pause.)

NICK: I have to tell you something

  (Pause.)

RUTH: Yes.

NICK: I thought that was what life was.

  (Pause.)

RUTH: What was?

  (Pause.)

NICK: To be still.

  (Pause.)

RUTH: Not to want a thing. I know.

NICK: To hear what did go on.
    And be content.

RUTH: Yes. It is like a brook. Yes.

NICK: Do you know?

RUTH: I do.

NICK: And be content.

RUTH *(pause):* Tell me one.

NICK: One what?

RUTH: A story.

NICK: No. I don't think that I ever tried to tell one.

RUTH: No?

NICK: Not one my father told.

RUTH: Or *any* one.

  (Pause.)

  Try.
  Or one he told you. Or about the Indians.

NICK: *I* don't know . . .

RUTH: Please. Please. You can. *(Pause.)* Please.
    I know that you know them.
    When you'd listen to them all those times.

  (Pause.)

  Please.

NICK: Alright.

RUTH: Oh, thank you. Good. This is the best.
   This is the best thing two people can do.
   To live through things together. If they share what
   they have done before.

   (NICK *prepares to tell story.*)

NICK: Have you ever fallen from great distances?

RUTH: What?

NICK: Have you ever fallen from great distances?

RUTH: This is the story?

NICK: Yes.

   (*Pause.*)

RUTH: Good. Go on.

   (*Pause.*)

   Go *on,* Nick.

   (*Pause.*)

NICK: I'm not sure I remember.

RUTH: Oh, don't tell me that. You do.

NICK: I want to tell it right.

RUTH: Well, tell it right, then. You can do it.

NICK: Would you think a man's life could be saved by
   someone's garter belt?

RUTH: A man's or woman's garter belt?

(Pause.)

NICK: Men do not wear garter belts.

RUTH: They didn't then, though?

NICK: No.

RUTH: To hold their socks up?

NICK: At their calves?

RUTH: Yes.

NICK: Those are just called "garters."

(Pause.)

RUTH: I'm sorry. Go on, Nicky. Yes. I would believe it.
Have I ever fallen from great distances and lived.
(Sotto, to self:) This is the story.

(Pause.)

NICK: In the War.
In The Black Forest.
Long ago.
My Dad went looking for a man he lost out on Patrol.
In Winter.

RUTH: Yes.

NICK: His name was Herman Waltz.

RUTH *(to self):* Waltz.

NICK: When the War was over, they would be involved
together.

RUTH: Uh-huh.

NICK: He was nuts.

RUTH: Waltz.

NICK: Yes.

RUTH: He was insane?

NICK: Yes. He thought his head was a radio.
He had had dental work and said that Hitler told him
things about his wife. Things he should do to her.
He later killed himself.

RUTH: When?

NICK: In the fifties.

(*Pause.*)

RUTH: And he's in this same story?

NICK: Yes.
He came up here. He said he had been kidnapped by
the Martians.

RUTH: No!

NICK: Yes.

RUTH: No.

NICK: He said he'd driven up . . .

RUTH: . . . Wait. Wait—he said the Martians kidnapped
him up *here* . . . ?

NICK: Yes.

RUTH: No.

NICK: He was on some road up here—he had come to see
my Dad, he saw the lights.

He told us he had fallen from great distances.
Inside their craft.

RUTH *(softly, to self):* No.

NICK: When they'd finished with him.

RUTH: No.

NICK: Yes.

(*Pause.*)

RUTH: And you saw this man?

NICK: I knew him. Yes.

RUTH *(to self):* He had been kidnapped by the Martians.

NICK: He said that he had.

RUTH: Did you believe him?

NICK: Yes.

(*Long pause.*)

RUTH *(softly):* I know.

NICK: He'd come up here . . . *(Pause.)* . . . he would be up here . . .

RUTH: Yes. In the War, too.

NICK: We do not know what goes on.

RUTH: I know we do not.

NICK: *Feelings, madness . . .*

RUTH *(softly):* Everything.

NICK: The *Indians.*

RUTH: That bear came back here.

NICK: That bear here?

RUTH: Yes.

NICK *(pause):* I'm sure it did.

RUTH: They built the house upon its cave and it came back.

NICK: I'm sure it did. These things go on.

RUTH: I know they do.

NICK: They all go on.

(*Pause.*)

All we have are insights.

(*Pause.*)

Who *knows* what's real?

RUTH: Yes.

NICK: They exist all independent of our efforts to explain them. Everything does. (*Pause.*) We cannot know it.

(*Pause.*)

My father. *Waltz.*

(*Pause.*)

They had *seen* things.

(Pause.)

Who knows. If they were real or not.

RUTH: Yes.

NICK: Whether they were real or not.

(Pause.)

He had had his insights.

(Pause.)

The things he saw. *(Pause.)* Whether he had imagined them or not. He had had insights.

(Pause.)

Do you know?

RUTH: Yes.

(Pause.)

NICK: You do?

RUTH: Yes.

(Pause.)

NICK: You know what I'm talking about?

RUTH: Yes. I believe these things.

(Pause.)

NICK: You see what I mean by his insights?

RUTH: Yes.

NICK: The *things* he'd seen.

RUTH: I know.

NICK: That Waltz had seen.

RUTH: But we don't have to be afraid.
    Because we have each other.

   (Pause.)

NICK: I'm not afraid.

RUTH: Of course you're not. But I meant if you *were*.
    As in a story. *(Pause.)*
    Because we have each other.

   (Pause.)

    Will you take me in the house?
    I want to lie down next to you.

   (Pause.)

    I want to hold you with my legs.
    I want to stick my fingers in you.
    I'm so glad we are here.
    When I am with you, Nick, I feel so strong.
    I feel like I know everything.

   (Pause.)

    I wish we could stay up here forever.

NICK: You wouldn't like it.

RUTH: No?

NICK: No.

RUTH: Yes, I would.

NICK: You'd be bored.

RUTH: No, I wouldn't. No.

(*Pause.*)

Why would I be bored?
I love it here.

NICK: Things change.

RUTH: In Winter?

NICK: Yes. In Winter. *Many* times.

RUTH: I know they do. That's why I like the country.
In the city we can never know each other really.

(*Pause.*)

It's clean out here.
And, plus, it's quiet.
Anything is possible. (*Pause.*)
You can see the way things are.

NICK: Like what?

RUTH: Like stars. (*Pause.*)
Like the way you look. (*Pause.*)
Many things. (*Pause.*)
Many things.
Can we go in now?

NICK: Yes. *(He gets up.)*

RUTH: And later, Nick . . . ?

NICK: What?

RUTH: I will give you something.

NICK: What?

RUTH: That I brought.

NICK: You brought something for me?

RUTH: Yes. A present.

NICK *(pause):* Thank you.

RUTH: Well.

(Pause.)

NICK: What is it?

RUTH: A surprise.

(Pause.)

Something for you. *(They start to walk in.)*
Wait! Oh, wait!
How did they find that man?

NICK: Who?

RUTH: Herman.

NICK: Herman Waltz.

RUTH: How did they find him?

(Pause.)

NICK: My Dad fell in a hole with him.

RUTH: No!

NICK: Yes.

(*Pause.*)

RUTH: Will you tell me?

(*Pause.*)

Because I have to know it.

NICK: Yes. I will.

RUTH: No. Do you promise?

NICK: Yes.

RUTH: Good. (*Pause.*) Oh! I'm so happy, Nick.
I never had a place like this.
With porches. (*They continue going in.*)

NICK: What did you bring me?

RUTH: You will have to wait till later. (*She turns back.*)
"They had fallen in a hole."

NICK: They did.

RUTH: Yes. (RUTH *turns. They go in.*)
You must tell me.

Scene 2

Night

Ruth *is sitting on a chair on the porch, looking out.* Nick *comes out.*

Nick *(enters):* My watch stopped.

Ruth: Can't you sleep?

Nick: What are you doing out here?

Ruth: Sitting.

Nick: Do you know what time it is?

Ruth: No.

  (Pause.)

Nick: My watch stopped.

Ruth: Can't you sleep?

Nick: No. I woke up.

  (Pause.)

Ruth: Are you restless?

46

NICK: I don't know what *time* it is . . .

RUTH: Come here. Come here.

> *(Pause. NICK goes to her reluctantly.)*

Did you have a bad dream?

NICK: No. I was not dreaming. No.

RUTH: Well, you're alright now.

> *(Pause.)*

NICK: I know.

RUTH: You're alright. *(She begins to rock him. She holds him.)* You are fine. *(Pause.)* Everything is just the way it should be.

NICK: I can't sleep.

RUTH: Why? Why, Babe?

NICK: *I* don't know.

RUTH: You want me to come back and hold you?

NICK: No.

RUTH: Alright.

NICK: It's cold. It's going to rain.

RUTH: I like it. I like Northern weather.

NICK: Why?

RUTH: It's clean.

> *(Pause.)*

NICK: I can't sleep.

RUTH: Do you want to take a walk?

NICK: Now?

RUTH: Yes.

(Pause.)

NICK: It's dark.

RUTH: It's night.

NICK: It's going to rain.
　　I don't want to go out there in the rain.

RUTH: We'll wear the rain things.

NICK: No. It's wet out there.

RUTH: Come on.

NICK: No.

RUTH: We'll go put the rain stuff on and go out to the Point.

NICK: No.

RUTH: Where the old rowboat is.

NICK: It isn't on the Point.

RUTH: It's not? The rowboat?

NICK: No.

RUTH: I saw it out there.

(Pause.)

NICK: The Point is over there. *(He points.)*

RUTH: That's where the rowboat is.

NICK: It is?

RUTH: Yes.

NICK: Then it's not our rowboat.

RUTH: No?

NICK: We kept our rowboat in the Cove.

RUTH: It's not your rowboat?

NICK: No.

RUTH: Oh.

(Pause.)

NICK: Is it blue?

RUTH: It's a kind of blue.

NICK: What is it?

RUTH: Green.
    It could of faded.

NICK: What's it called?

RUTH: I don't know.

NICK: Did you see a name on it?

RUTH: No. I don't think so.

NICK: On the transom?

RUTH: Near the back? The transom's near the back?

(Pause.)

The transom is the stern. Right, Nicky?

NICK: Yes.

RUTH: It's gone. It doesn't have one.
It got rotted off. I told you.

(Pause.)

What was yours called?

NICK: I don't remember.

RUTH: Let's go take a walk. We'll put the stuff on. Boots
and stuff.

NICK: There's lightning.

RUTH: No, there isn't.

NICK: Well, there will be.

RUTH: I don't think it's coming here.

NICK: You don't.

RUTH: No. And it cannot kill you.

NICK: It can't.

RUTH: No.

NICK: You think that it can't kill you?

RUTH: No. It isn't going to hit you.
Come on, Nicky.

NICK: I do not want to get wet.

RUTH: You won't.

NICK: I'm wet now, Ruth; it's blowing.

(Pause.)

RUTH: Nick. It's lovely.
It is poetry.
The damp.
You know what this is? Bracing.
Come on. We'll put stuff on and you'll like it.
It will be nice by the Point.

NICK: It's night.

RUTH: That's alright.
Are you hungry?

NICK: No.

RUTH: Well, I could put food on, and we'll go out and we'll
come back here and eat.
We'll have an appetite.

(Pause.)

We'll feel good.

(Pause.)

But we don't have to.

NICK: If you want to, take a walk. It's alright.

RUTH: Come *on*, Nick, I don't want to take one by *myself*,
for chrissake. *(Pause.)*
I want to be with *you* out there.
It will be wet, but we will not be *getting* wet. Our faces,
just. The two of us.
I always thought, I always wanted it to be like this.

(Pause.)

With my lover. In the country.
In the middle of the night. This is so beautiful.
Here we're awake. All by ourselves.
Oh, Nicky. All alone.

(Pause.)

NICK: I'm glad that you're happy.

(Pause.)

RUTH: Drip, drip, drip. The snow makes sound, too. Do
you think?

NICK: I don't know.

RUTH: We could sit out here in Winter. We could watch
the snow come down. Huh?
What about that?
Bundled up in coats and blankets with our scarf
around our neck and stocking hats. Huh?

(Pause.)

Wouldn't that be funny?

NICK: Yes, that would.

RUTH: Just sitting out here in the Winter.
Bundled up. Not moving.
Like some married couple in a picture.
Rocking back and forth.

(Pause.)

Come here. Come here.
Oh, you're sleepy.
Come here and I'll tell a story. *(He moves close to her.)*
I will tell a story and then we can go to sleep.
I'm going to tell a bedtime story.

NICK: Alright.

RUTH: That my Grandmother told me.
You would of loved her. I think.
She was old.

NICK: How old was she?

RUTH: Well, she was old. When she died, she was eighty-
six.
She saw a lot of things.
She always told us bedtime stories.
And then we would go to sleep.
Come here.

NICK: Is it wet?

RUTH: No. No. I'm going to keep you dry.

NICK: I'll get wet.

RUTH: No, you won't.

NICK: It's going to blow all over me.

RUTH: I'll shield you, come here. *(Pause.)*
It's going to blow the other way.

NICK: How do you know?

RUTH: I know.

NICK: How?

RUTH: Because I just know. *(Pause. He goes to her.)*

RUTH: Now, this feels better. We could never do this in the city. Are you comfortable?

NICK: Yes.

RUTH: Good.

(Pause.)

There was the moon and wolves and these old women and small children.

NICK *(softly):* It's dry here.

RUTH: I told you.
And there always was a moon . . .
A crescent moon . . . a new moon . . .
What's a new moon?

NICK: I don't know.

RUTH: Does it mean big or small?

NICK: I don't know.

(Pause.)

RUTH: And I was always in them. And my brother.
She would tell us—now relax.
One day at dinnertime, these children had gone to their Granma's house. They loved her very much.
While she was cooking, they asked could they go and play—the house was near the woods—and she said yes, they could, but that they had these *wolves* in them, and bears lived in them, too.

NICK: Some brown bears.

RUTH: Yes.

NICK: Some European Brown Bears.

RUTH: Now, be quiet. So we must be careful in the woods.
    We had to take care of each other, and be very careful
    not to go too far.
    The moon came up. The breezes blew.
    The sun was going down.
    The little children went into the woods.
    It became cold.
    They found that they had lost their way.
    They could not see the moon.
    Birds called to one another.

(Pause.)

"The Sun is Down."
The rain began to fall . . .
Oh, Nicky, are you sleeping?

NICK: No.

RUTH: You want to take a walk?

NICK: No.

(Pause.)

I have to ask you something.

RUTH: What?

NICK: Do you like it up here?

RUTH: Yes.

(Pause.)

NICK: What happened when you got there?

RUTH: When we got inside?

NICK: Yes.

RUTH: In the woods . . .
    We became lost.
    We lost our way. *(To self:)* The sun is down, the rain
    began to fall. *(Aloud:)* I think that always at the end our
    parents found us in the morning.

    (Pause.)

    Although I don't remember.

NICK: Is she dead now?

RUTH: Granma?
    Yes. She died.

    (Pause.)

NICK: Do you miss her?

RUTH: Very much. I miss her all the time.
    I think about her. *(Pause.)*
    I lost her bracelet. That her husband gave her.
    Well, I told you.

    (Pause.)

    I dropped it in the Lake.
    I can still see it.
    Falling.
    Falling.
    Are you cold?

NICK: A little.

(Pause.)

My father fell into this old abandoned mine with Herman Waltz.

RUTH: Uh-huh.

NICK: Waltz told him that they'd never leave that hole alive.

RUTH: And how deep was it?

NICK: Deep. Deep. Very deep.

RUTH: Did they have stuff to eat?

NICK: No. *(Pause.)* And they were cold.

RUTH: I *bet* they were.

NICK: And battered.

(Pause.)

RUTH: How long did they stay down there?

NICK: And the rain fell.

(Pause.)

RUTH: And they were down there how long?

(Pause.)

NICK: They got out that afternoon.

RUTH: Oh.

(Pause.)

NICK: The rescue party found them.

RUTH: Mmm.

NICK: It rained the whole time.

RUTH: Many times the best and worst things happen over just a little while.

NICK: My Dad said all he talked about was his new wife.

RUTH: Waltz.

NICK: In Chicago. How he'd never see his wife again.

RUTH: Sometimes when you stay up you get these visions.

NICK: Do you want a drink?

RUTH: Sure.

(NICK *goes inside.*)

NICK *(from inside):* When he got back to Chicago, he would beat her up.

RUTH: What?

(*Pause.* NICK *comes out with bottle.*)

NICK: He used to beat her up.

RUTH: He used to beat his *wife* up?

NICK: Yes.

(*Pause.*)

RUTH: Why?

NICK: I don't know.

RUTH: Oh.

(Pause.)

NICK: He was crazy.

RUTH *(to self):* Yes.

NICK: My Dad said he was an unhappy man.

RUTH: This is the man that saw the Martians.

NICK: Yes.

RUTH: He said he saw them here.

NICK: Near here.

RUTH *(to self):* Actually right near here. *(Pause. She drinks.)*
I like this stuff.

NICK: Uh-huh.

RUTH: My Granma never slept.
She had this couch out by the window and she had a
quilt.

(NICK *takes bottle.*)

She'd keep the window open. We were on the first
floor. Sometimes I would see her in the morning, all
wrapped up in her quilt and looking out the window.
She would tell these stories.
They had Cossacks.
They had bears there.
People were escaping and she hid them underneath
her petticoats. They took them all to safety through
the Forest.

(Pause.)

NICK *(to self):* That *could* of been our rowboat . . .

RUTH: She loved her husband very much.
   He was killed.

NICK: What was he?

RUTH: A blacksmith. He was older than her.

NICK: What did he die of?

RUTH: He was killed. I used to ask my mother how come
   she was sitting in the window.
   She just sat there. Granma.
   She would tell me, in the Winter, they would make
   love. Him and her. For hours.

NICK: Your grandmother told you?

RUTH: Yes.

NICK: How old were you?

RUTH: I don't know.
   They would lay in bed.
   I saw the Photographs of what she looked like. And of
   him.
   When she was little, too.
   She looked like me.
   She said he was like Iron. He could lift her in one
   hand.
   They'd lie in bed all day and never speak . . . they'd
   take long walks.

(Pause.)

Oh, she told me many times. The way his hair smelled.
In the rain.
The singed forearms. The smell . . .

(Pause.)

Granma married this man in Chicago.

(Pause.)

He was a nice man. Jacky Weiss.

(Pause.)

But she missed her husband so. She used to watch the
window in the snow. It was cold. You could hear her
whispering. I don't know. Maybe she was praying.

(Pause.)

She loved him. They were married.
Nothing, even he was crippled—or she was—could
separate them.
She was his. Forever.
They had made a vow.

NICK *(to self):* Some pagan vow.

(Pause.)

RUTH: He gave that necklace to her.
  Can you think, Nick?
  All the secrets, all the things they shared?
  At night. In bed.

(Pause.)

She was like the Earth.
She knew so many things.
I think about her all the time.
I wish I had not lost her bracelet.

(Pause.)

She used to wear it.

(Pause.)

NICK: Who killed him?

RUTH: I don't know.
Some farmer.

(She takes wine. Drinks.)

(She declaims:) Wine, wine, wine.
The Earth. The Sky. The Rain.

NICK: The Water.

RUTH: Yes.

(Pause.)

NICK: Women are immortal.

RUTH: No. They have no sense of values.
No, I know.

(Pause. She goes over to an oar.)

An oar. What is this? It goes in the oarlock. What is
it called?

NICK: An oarlock pin.

(Pause.)

RUTH (to self): Oarlock pin.
This thing could be the color of the boat. This is from
your boat?

NICK: Yes.

RUTH: Then I think it's the same one. I think it is.

NICK: It's going to come down.

RUTH: To really come down.

NICK: Yes.

RUTH: The rain.
The water brings the fishes out.

(Pause.)

After the rain they huddle near the surface.

(Pause.)

And then you can catch them.
Fish come up for insects. When the storm is over.

NICK: For the larvae.

RUTH: Larvae?

NICK: Yes.

RUTH: The little insects?

NICK: Yes.

RUTH: The fish come up to eat them?

NICK: Yes.

RUTH: I know they do.

> *(Pause.)*

> Drip drip. Rain comes down, drip. It makes rings. It makes these circles.
> *Ripples.* Plop. A fish comes up. Fishes come up. They make the same ripples from underneath.

> *(Pause.)*

NICK: Larvae are really eggs.

RUTH: I know that.

> *(Pause.)*

> I used to say that we are only fish beneath the sea. I read this book when I was small—it said that we live in an ocean made of air and we are only fish beneath the sea.

NICK: You said that?

RUTH: Yes. You know, except we couldn't *swim* or anything. *(Pause.)* You want to come with on my walk?

> *(Big lightning flash.)*

> Look at *that!*

NICK: Lightning.

RUTH: Jesus, Nicky, huh?

NICK *(to self):* A storm.

RUTH: I bet that you watched them a lot. Storms.
If I was out here, I would sit all day.
I would.
We always used to know, it rained, the thing we had
to do was go and put the boats onto their side. To turn
them upside-down.
You know?
You ever sit inside a boat that way?
Some rowboat or canoe?

NICK: Yes.

   (Pause.)

RUTH: It's nice.

NICK: Yes.

RUTH: All *warm* . . .
Look at that!
The wind howls and howls, but you're warm.

NICK: I'd sit here.

RUTH: Yes.

NICK: And think about things like that.

RUTH: Would you? *(Pause.)* What things?

NICK: You know.

   (Pause.)

RUTH: Tell me.

NICK: Homes and things.

RUTH: When the storms blew.

NICK: Yes.

RUTH: What about them?

NICK: Living in them. Being warm.

(*Pause.*)

RUTH: Being in them with somebody.

NICK: Yes.

RUTH: Please tell me.

NICK: I don't know.

(*Pause.*)

RUTH: Tell me.

NICK: Just these thoughts I had.

RUTH: When you would settle down.

NICK: Yes.

RUTH: Here?

NICK: I don't know.

RUTH: Who with?

(*Pause.*)

NICK: I don't know.

RUTH: And what would you think?

NICK: How it would be.

RUTH: How would it be?

NICK: I don't know.

RUTH: Yes. You do. Tell me.

NICK: I don't know.

RUTH: Please tell me. *(Pause.)* Please tell me. *(Pause.)* *Please.*

   (Pause.)

NICK: We would meet.

RUTH: Uh-huh.

NICK: And . . . you know, we would meet and we would just be happy.

RUTH: You would.

NICK: Yes.

   (Pause.)

RUTH: What, with Houses?

NICK: Yes.

RUTH: Here?

NICK: No.

   (Pause.)

RUTH: *Some*where.

NICK: Yes. And maybe it was raining.

RUTH: It was raining?

NICK: In my dream.

RUTH: When you would be with someone.

(Pause.)

NICK: Do you think that is childish?

RUTH: What?

NICK: *Day*dreaming.

RUTH: No.

NICK: You don't?

RUTH: Not if you thought it. *(Pause.)* But sometimes things are different than the way you thought they'd be when you set out on them.
This doesn't mean that, *you* know, that they aren't . . . that they aren't . . . Wait. Do you know what I mean?

NICK: No.

RUTH: That they aren't *good.*
Just because they're different.

(Pause.)

NICK: What's your surprise?

RUTH: Things can be unexpected and be beautiful if we will let them. *(Pause.)* And not be frightened by them, Nick.

NICK: What did you bring me?

RUTH: I will tell you later.
  Do you understand me?

NICK: No.

RUTH: You do, though.

  (Pause.)

You don't have to be nervous when a thing is new.

NICK: I am not nervous.

RUTH: No, but that is all I mean. *(Pause.)* Sometimes things
  are different.

  (Pause.)

NICK: This drink is good.

RUTH: I know. Drink it. It's good.
  Do you know what I mean?
  We all have fantasies.
  And dreams.
  I have them.
  Many things I want.

  (Pause.)

Or would dream about.
  I know they can be frightening.
  To do them.

  (Pause.)

I know.

David Mamet

NICK: You know that, eh?

   (Pause.)

RUTH: What?

   (Pause.)

   (Lightning flash.)

   The lightning doesn't look like anything.
   Do you know what I mean?

NICK: No.

   (Pause.)

RUTH: It doesn't "look" like anything.

   (Pause.)

   Do you know what I mean?

NICK: No. *(He chuckles.)*

RUTH: What's funny?

NICK: Nothing.

RUTH: All I meant, like clouds, or something.
   They look like something.
   You know what I meant.

NICK: I'm sorry.

   (Pause.)

RUTH: I wasn't trying to be funny.

NICK: I know.

RUTH: Then you shouldn't *laugh* at me.
Do you think that I'm funny? Huh?
I know I'm funny *sometimes* . . .

(Pause.)

There's nothing wrong in being serious.

NICK: I'm sorry.

(Pause.)

RUTH: It's alright.

(Pause.)

I understand. *(She starts to go.)*

NICK: You going?

RUTH: Yes.

NICK: Hold on. I'm sorry.

RUTH: I'm just going for my walk.

NICK: Where are you going?

RUTH: By the Lake.

NICK: Come here a minute.

RUTH: What?

NICK: Come here.

RUTH: I'll be back in a while.
　　I'll be right back. *(Pause.)* I'm getting sticky in this suit
　　if I'm not in the rain.

NICK: Come here.
　　I want to tell you something. Sit down.

(Pause.)

RUTH: You want me to sit down now?

NICK: Yes.

RUTH: Alright. *(She sits down.)*

NICK: I'm sorry that I laughed at you.

RUTH: No. That's alright. I understand. *(She gets up to go.)*

NICK: Hold on.

RUTH: I'll be back. I just want to be out there with the
　　lightning.

NICK: Come here. *(He begins to pull her down to the floor.)*

RUTH: What? It's wet. (NICK *begins making sexual overtures.)*

NICK: Mmm.

RUTH: It's wet. This stuff is sticky.

NICK: You smell good.

RUTH: I was out in the sun today. Come on, the floor is
　　wet, Nick.

NICK: Lift up.

RUTH: I'll be back. Just let me go, and I'll come back.

NICK: Come on.

RUTH: Alright. We'll go inside. *(She starts to get up.)*

NICK: Lift up a minute.

RUTH: Wait. Hold on. We'll go inside.

NICK: This is all knotted.

RUTH: Hold on, Nick.

(He tears her pants off.)

You tore 'em, will you hold *on,* for chrissake? This thing is rough.

(He kicks over the bottle.)

You're knocking the *bottle.*
Alright. Alright.
Wait.
Just hold on a second.

(He pushes the rainshell up over her face.)

Just a second. Oh. Okay. Hold on a second, though.

(He prepares to mount her.)

No, *wait!*
Wait.
I can't *see!*
No. Wait. *(She fights the shell down and maneuvers a little way away from him.)*

(Pause.)

I'll go inside. I'll get some stuff.

(Pause.)

Do you want me to go get some stuff? *(Pause.)*

NICK *(of rainwear):* This shit is all mildewed.

RUTH: Do you want me to go in and get some stuff?

NICK *(to self):* How can you wear this?

RUTH: I'll go right in and get it.

(Pause.)

I'll get the stuff.

NICK: No.

RUTH: I will.

NICK: No.

RUTH: Are you sure?

(Pause.)

NICK: Where's the bottle?

RUTH: I don't know. *(She looks for bottle.)*

NICK: Do you know, there's nothing to do here.

RUTH: Well, that isn't my fault, Nicky.

NICK: I didn't say it was your fault.

RUTH: Yes. You did. There's lots to do here.
      We could walk around. I walked around.

There's lots to do. You said that you liked thunder-storms. There's lots of things to do. Don't tell me that.

(*Pause.*)

You're mad because I wasn't wet.

NICK: No. I'm not.

RUTH: You are. You pushed me, though.

NICK: I'm sorry.

RUTH (*to self*): Yeah.

NICK: I'm sorry.

(*Pause.*)

RUTH: You can't, just because you know, just because you *want* something. . . . There is a way things are.

NICK: Mmm.

RUTH: You know?

NICK: No. What in the world are you talking about?

RUTH: That you're mad 'cause I wasn't wet.

NICK: That isn't true.

RUTH: You think that means I do not want you.

NICK: No.

RUTH: You do.

NICK: I know that it doesn't mean that.

RUTH: No, you don't.

NICK: I do.

RUTH: Yeah?

NICK: I know that you want me.

RUTH: I *do* want you.

NICK: I know that.

RUTH: But you just can't push me *around.*

NICK: I know.

RUTH: You don't. You're all inside this thing you're in. A shell, or something. You can't see. This is no good. No. If you come up here with me, that means you are . . .

(Pause.)

NICK: What?

RUTH: What? Nothing.

NICK: What did you say?

(Pause.)

RUTH: I didn't.

NICK: Yes, you did. What did you say? *(Pause.)* You tell me what you said.

RUTH: I said—I said—that when you come up here that means you are committed.

NICK: Oh.

RUTH: Yes. If you are a man. Because I am your guest.

NICK *(to self):* If I'm a man.

RUTH: And you know how I want you, so don't tell me you're mad that I'm not wet. Don't tell me that. But you, you do not treat me with respect.

NICK: Will you shut up one second, please?

(Pause.)

You talk too much, Ruth.

RUTH: I don't.

NICK: Why don't you take your walk?

RUTH: Why don't *you?*

(Pause.)

I'll shut up, you want me to shut up?
I'll shut up. *(Pause. Of oar:)* Why is this all burnt?

NICK: I used to use it in the Winters when I stirred the fire up.

RUTH: When you would *come* up here.

(Pause.)

NICK: Yes.

RUTH: When you would come up here with other people.

(Pause.)

NICK: Yes.

RUTH: Oh.

(Pause.)

You frightened me.

NICK: I'm sorry.

RUTH: I came here, and then you acted funny.
    I thought that we were both in this together.

(NICK drinks.)

May I have some? *(He gives her wine. Pause.)*

NICK: I'm sorry.

RUTH: Yeah. Oh, well. That's alright. These things have
    to come out.

(Pause.)

NICK: I'm sorry, Ruth.

RUTH: Okay. *(They sit down.)*

NICK: What have you got for me?

RUTH: I have a lot of things for you. I have so many things.
    You don't know. I'm not who you think I am, Nick.

(Pause.)

NICK: What is the present?

(Pause.)

I meant the present.

RUTH: I know what you mean. I am not stupid. Do you want it?

NICK: Yes.

RUTH: Are you sure?

NICK: Yes.

RUTH: Alright.

NICK: What is it?

RUTH: I am going to give it to you. *(She gets up.)*

NICK: Wait.

RUTH: What?

NICK: I don't know.

RUTH: What? *(Pause.)* You don't know what?

NICK: I don't know if I want it.

RUTH: Oh.

(Pause.)

Oh.
You are so dumb sometimes. My God.
You are so dumb.

NICK: All of this *rain* . . .

RUTH: Well, it's *raining.* That's got nothing to do, rain, with anything.

NICK: We sat out here.

RUTH *(to self)*: We're sitting out here *now* . . .

NICK: And read.

RUTH: You read books.

NICK: Or told stories. We came up here with our friends.

(*Pause.*)

RUTH: Are you lonely?

NICK: I would look up at the stars.

RUTH: Uh-huh. (*Pause.*) Are you lonely?

NICK: I don't know.

(*Pause.*)

RUTH: Do you want me to go home?

NICK: I don't know.

(*Pause.*)

RUTH: Why can't you sleep?

NICK: I don't know.

RUTH: Yes. You do. What is it?

NICK: Nothing.

RUTH: Yes, it is. (*Pause.*) Tell me.

NICK: No, it's not anything. I'm sorry . . .
Come here . . .

RUTH: Are you mad at me?

NICK: No.

RUTH: Do you want to go in?

NICK: No.

(Pause.)

RUTH: What *do* you want?

(Pause.)

Come on, we'll go inside.

NICK: Why?

RUTH: I don't know. We'll make a sandwich.

NICK: Why?

RUTH: Because if you were hungry.

NICK: Well, I'm not.

RUTH: Okay. Okay. We have to talk.
I have to talk to you. (Pause.)
Gimme some.

NICK: You're drunk.

RUTH: I am not. Gimme some. (He gives her some wine.)
Alright. Siddown. Look: Are you cold?

NICK: Yes.

RUTH: Alright, then. Look. You stay here.
I am going to get you something.
Stay here. (She goes inside, and comes out and hands him a package.) This is for you.

(Pause.)

NICK: What is it?

RUTH: Just open it. *(Pause.)*
Open it, and then we'll talk.

(He opens it. He takes out a bracelet. He examines it.)

NICK: It's very nice. *(Pause. He continues to examine the bracelet.)* Is it gold?

(Pause.)

RUTH: Read it.

NICK: "Nicholas. *(Pause.)* I will always love you. Ruth."

(A long pause.)

RUTH: Put it on.

NICK *(very softly):* No.

RUTH: Then go fuck yourself. Look: You don't understand. You don't know me. You don't.
You think that I'm stupid. You do.
You think that. *Don't* you?

NICK: No.

RUTH: Yeah, you do. You don't know, you don't know a thing. Look. Look. Look, Nick.
I love you. I love you so much. I just want to be with you. That's the only thing I want to do. I do not want to hurt you.

(Pause.)

Do you want to make love to me?
Nick?
Do you want to make love?

(Pause.)

NICK: No.

(Pause.)

RUTH: You don't want to make love to me?

NICK: No.

RUTH: You know that I want you, Nick. You know that.

(Pause.)

Why do you think I came up with you?

NICK: Why?

RUTH: Do you *care?*

NICK: Why did you come up?

RUTH: You don't know why I did? Are you *dumb?*
What do you mean?

(Pause.)

Caw, caw, caw, the gulls fly.
They eat fish?

NICK: I don't know.

RUTH: They either eat the fish or insects. *(Pause.)*
We eat fish. The fish eat seaweed.
It all dies, the things turn into shells.

(Pause.)

Or deposits. They wash up. As coral.
Maybe they make sand, or special beaches.
They decay and wash away.

(Pause.)

Then they form the islands.

(Pause.)

Nothing lasts forever.

(Pause.)

Don't make me go home.

(Pause.)

I want to live with you. Go put it on.

NICK: I know some things that you don't know.

RUTH: You know what?

NICK: Things.

RUTH: Things.

(Pause.)

You don't know *any*thing.

(Pause.)

You don't even know what's *good* for you, you come up
here with all those others, I don't know, and the only
woman who loves you and you don't know *shit.* You
think I'm stupid.

(Pause.)

You never had this. *You're* the one that's stupid.

NICK: Do you know that you demean yourself?

RUTH: I do.

NICK: Yes.

RUTH: Isn't that too bad.

NICK: It is.

RUTH: You don't have any feelings.

NICK: I have feelings.

RUTH: What are they?

(Pause.)

What are they?
You *think* that you have feelings.
Why do we come up here if you're so upset the whole
time, that's what I would like to know.

NICK: Why?

(Pause.)

RUTH: You *asked* me, I am your guest up here.
You're bored or what, what am I s'posed to do, go off
and drown myself somewhere?

I am your guest.
We could be many things to one another.

(Pause.)

In our friendship.
You have no idea of the possibilities.

(Pause.)

Do you know that?

NICK: Why don't you leave me alone?

(Pause.)

RUTH: I will. *(Pause.)* I don't like to be in places where I
don't feel good.
When's the next bus?

NICK: In the morning.

RUTH: Well, I'm going to take it. So that's it.
So you can just relax. I've had enough of this. *(Pause.)*
Life goes on.
Drip *drip.*
Drip *drip.*
Do you feel better now?

NICK: Yes.

RUTH: Good. *(Pause.)* I care how you feel.
We have to learn from things. *(Pause.)* Do you think
that?

NICK: Yes. I do.

RUTH: Yes, I do, too. *(Pause.)*
　　Many things go on.
　　We have to learn from them. Good. Good.
　　Your friend saw Martians here.

NICK: My father's friend.

RUTH: You think that there are Martians?

NICK: On Earth?

RUTH: Yes.

NICK: There might be.

RUTH: But what do you *think?*

NICK: I don't know, Ruth.

RUTH: Inside our ocean made of air?

NICK: I don't know, for God's sake. *(He gets up.)*

RUTH: What would you do if you, you know, if you came
　　across them?
　　You think you'd be scared?

(Pause.)

　　If you saw a Martian?
　　Or a ghost.
　　Some vision?

NICK: Of what?

RUTH: I don't know.
　　You said that you thought they came among us.
　　They could do that.
　　They could infiltrate our people.

NICK: I am getting wet.

RUTH: Please. I have to ask you, they could monitor us.
They could send down members of their company to
live here.
They would look like you and me.

(NICK *gets up and starts to go in.*)

Please. Wait. I'm telling you.
I'm telling you this story.
We would come into the kitchen, we would hang our
hat up, "Hi, Babe . . . did you have a good day?"
But there wouldn't be an answer.

(*Pause.* NICK *gets up.*)

Please, please, I have to tell you this.
Because there was no one *there.*

(*Pause.*)

They played upon us.
We had been alone the whole time.
We had wanted it for so long that they came and they
knew our desires.
There was no one there.

(*Pause.* NICK *shakes his head.*)

What?

NICK: You have no idea what you're saying.

RUTH: I don't.

NICK: Not at all.

(Pause.)

Not at all.

(Pause. They sit for a moment then she gets up to go in.)

Where are you going?

RUTH: In. I have to pack.

Scene 3

Morning

Ruth: It's rotten when you don't feel good. I know.

(Pause.)

Do you want some more coffee?

Nick: No.

(Pause.)

Ruth: Would you like to take a walk?

Nick: It's all wet.

Ruth: We could put our boots on.

Nick: I don't think so.

(Pause.)

Ruth *(of jacket):* Your Dad wore this in the War, huh?

Nick: No. I don't feel good.

Ruth: I know.

NICK: He wore another one.

RUTH: We could go down by the Point. Down there. *(Of oar:)* Do these things float?

NICK: Unless they're waterlogged.

RUTH: Is this one?

NICK: No. It's burnt.

RUTH: You're tired.

NICK: Yes.

RUTH: Well, later you can take a nap.

NICK: I think I will.

RUTH: If we go to take a walk, you might get tired out.

NICK: No. Please, no.

RUTH: I'm sorry.

(Pause.)

NICK: I'm not glad that you're going.

RUTH: We don't have to become morbid.

NICK: We can see each other.

RUTH: Back there?

NICK: Yes.

(Pause.)

RUTH: Nicky, Nicky, Nicky.

NICK: No?

(Pause.)

We used to have all these different animals up here.

RUTH: Uh-huh.

NICK: Blue herons. Beavers.

RUTH: I don't think that you had beavers here.

NICK: Well, we did. The herons flew along.
They flew along at sunset. I would watch them.

RUTH: Herons. They still have them?

NICK: I don't know. They fly so slowly.
And their wings touch down and make two circles.

RUTH: Mmm.

NICK: Their feet drag.

(Pause.)

We caught this raccoon one time in a milk crate.

(Pause.)

RUTH: You told me.

NICK: Yes.

(Pause.)

I'll call you up.

(Pause.)

I'll call you when you get back.

RUTH: Mm.

NICK: No?

RUTH: Come on.

NICK: What?

RUTH: You know.

NICK: What?

RUTH: Nothing changes just because you move it somewhere else.

NICK: I'll call you.

RUTH: Yeah. Don't.

(Pause.)

I'm sorry.

NICK: Alright.

RUTH: You know. It gets cold.

NICK: Mm.

RUTH: We put clothes on.

NICK: Uh-huh.

RUTH: Yes. I've got to tell you: We put on clothes, we can
not make out what we look like.

(Pause.)

We make mistakes. We all get guarded.

(Pause.)

It's very lonely, and we all get desperate to be warm.
We have to find our lovers when it's warm.
We look at people and we see the things they are.
When they are on the Beach, or when they're happy.

(Pause.)

Some things that look like maybe they'd be good for
us.

(Pause.)

It gets real cold up here until the fog burns off.

NICK: Mmm.

RUTH: You need insulation.

NICK: Well, we're right up on the Lake.

(Pause.)

RUTH: Yes.

(Pause.)

NICK: We had talked about it at one time.

RUTH: The thing about fish, they stay down there, it makes
no difference to them.

NICK: Waves don't make a difference.

RUTH: What?

NICK: The waves don't make a difference.

(Pause.)

They're on the surface, but they don't affect the water underneath.

RUTH: They don't?

NICK: No.

RUTH: Currents, only, right?

(Pause.)

I don't know, I don't know.
Everything gets over.

(Pause.)

You know?
We all try to be very brave. What do you call it when you try not to show anything?

NICK: I don't know.

(Pause.)

RUTH: We all try to be warriors. Or pirates, something. They all used to go to sea and rape the cabin boys. The Vikings.

(Pause.)

The worst part, maybe, is just learning little *things.* The *things* about each other. Other people.

(Pause.)

e if they play the piano.
til you have taken care of them when they are sick.
he way their sweat tastes.

(Pause.)

Those are the worst things.

NICK: We could call each other up.

RUTH: Oh, you're so sorry sometimes.

NICK: I am.

RUTH: Yes.

NICK: Do you want some more coffee?

RUTH: No.

NICK: You have a hangover?

RUTH: No.

NICK: Do we have an aspirin?

RUTH: I don't know.

NICK: You hungry?

RUTH: No. Are you?

NICK: I don't know.

RUTH: I might have an aspirin in my bag.

NICK: It's all packed.

RUTH: I'll get it.

NICK: No. What time is it?

RUTH: Eight-thirty.

(Pause.)

NICK: Do you want to go inside and lie down for a while?

RUTH: No.

NICK: Did you get any sleep?

RUTH: I didn't want to sleep.

NICK: You could go in and take a nap. I'll wake you.

RUTH: I can nap on the way back.

NICK: What will you do when you get back?

RUTH: I don't know.

NICK: Do you want to call me up to tell me you got in alright?

RUTH: No.

NICK: Did you take your wet stuff?

RUTH: Yes.

NICK: There's any stuff you want to leave, I'll bring it in.

RUTH: Why would I want to leave it?

(Pause.)

NICK: To dry.

RUTH: It's alright.

NICK: Call me up tonight to tell me you got in alright.

RUTH: I have things that I have to do.

NICK: Oh.

(Pause.)

I'll think about you.

RUTH: Will you.

NICK: Yes.

RUTH: You'll think about me while you're here.

NICK: Yes.

(Pause.)

RUTH: I bet.

NICK: I will.

RUTH: The gulls fly. Caw, Caw, Caw. And Winter comes
and they go somewhere else.
Do they go somewhere else when Winter comes?

NICK: I don't know.

RUTH: You were up here.

NICK: Well, I don't remember.

RUTH: All the times that you came up here?

NICK: I didn't come up here that many times.

RUTH: No, huh?

NICK: No.

RUTH: In Winter.

NICK: No.

RUTH: With all your little memories.

NICK: What memories?

RUTH: About things.

NICK: What things?

RUTH: Everything. I don't know. *(Pause.)* I'm going swimming.

NICK: It's too cold.

RUTH: It's not. The water still stays warm.

NICK: The air.

RUTH: I'll dry off.

NICK: It might rain again.

RUTH: Uh-huh. What? Lightning's going to kill me?

(Pause.)

NICK: Why are you going swimming?

RUTH: To wake up.

NICK: It's filthy. All the beach is mud.
The water is all muddy. *(Pause.)* Huh?

RUTH: Just leave me to be by myself for a minute.

NICK: You want me to come with you?

RUTH: No.

NICK: You sure?

RUTH: I'm, yeah, I'm sure. Yeah. What time is it?

NICK: Your suit will be cold.

RUTH: Mm.

NICK: Don't wear it, it will just get wet again.

RUTH: You want me to go down there naked?

NICK: Yes.

RUTH: Fuck you.

(*Pause.*)

NICK: Why do you say that?

RUTH: I don't have to tell you.

NICK: What, your body? (*Pause.*)
I want to see your body?
That's why I tell you to go down there?

(*Pause.*)

I can see your body anytime I want to.
Isn't that a little bit ridiculous?
Don't you think that that's a little silly?

RUTH (*pause*): If you say so.

NICK: I can see your body anytime I want to. (*Pause.*)
Can't I?

RUTH: You know that is all gone, Nicky.

NICK: That's all gone?

RUTH: That is all over now.

NICK: It is?

RUTH: You know it is. If I stay in too long, will you call
down for me?

NICK: Stay here a second.

RUTH: What? I'm freezing, what?

NICK: Come here.

RUTH: What?

NICK: Just come here. I want to talk to you.

RUTH: Come *on* now, Nicky.

NICK: Come here.

RUTH: Oh, just *stop* it, huh? Just *stop* it.

NICK: What?

RUTH: Grow up. *(He goes to her.)*

NICK: Does that feel good?

RUTH: Please.

NICK: Doesn't that feel good?

RUTH: For Christ's sake, *stop* it!

NICK: Let's go upstairs.

RUTH: Come on, Nick.

NICK: Let's do it.

RUTH: I'm—just grow up—I am going swimming. *Please.*
(She moves away from him.)

NICK: Come upstairs with me.

RUTH: Will you come and call me in a half an hour?

NICK: I want you to come upstairs with me. I want to fuck
you.

(Pause.)

RUTH: That's charming.

NICK: Is it?

RUTH: Yes. It is.

NICK: I want to fuck you.

RUTH: Well, you just go fuck your*self.* I'm going swimming.

NICK: What did you say?

RUTH: I said you can fuck your *own* self.

NICK *(pause):* You're so full of shit.

RUTH: I'm what?

NICK: Okay. Okay. Go.

RUTH: What? I'm full of shit?

NICK: Go. Go on. Go. I'll call you. *(Pause.)* Go in the water.

RUTH: Wait. I'm full of shit about what? *(Pause.)*
You have bizarre ideas, you know? *(Pause.)*
With your fantasies. You're goddamn *right* go fuck
yourself.
Go up here all the time—I don't know—some poor
babe you get to come here you can stick your fingers
in them and you tell them how Your Father Fought in
World War Two.
And those dumb Martians. You're so fucking corny.
You don't belong *here* . . .
You don't even know the things are *good* for you.
You do not know what's going *on* . . . *(Pause.)*
Your father and that guy they sat—You're so afraid of
everything—
You make this manly stuff up . . .

Him and that guy with the Martians, they were going
to die.
Inside that hole.
What did they *think* of?
When they talked about their broads.
When they were going to die?
You stupid shit.
. . . sucking each other off inside that hole . . .
Who did they *think* of?

(Pause.)

When they were dead?
You stupid shit.

NICK: Shut up.

RUTH: There *are* no men.

NICK: Shut up.

RUTH: You don't know *dick.* And I respected you, too. *(She
snorts.)* You lure the poor babes up here in the Winter
and you roll around and tell them of the Indians. You
fuck them and you send them home.
I hope you're very happy. *(Pause.)* You don't deserve
me.

NICK: Me. I don't deserve you.

RUTH: No. You don't.

NICK: You're *nothing,* honey.

RUTH: YES, I AM.

NICK: You're nothing with your cheapjack shit.
(He throws bracelet which has been on table down to floor.)

This talk is cheap. This sentiment.
You're *nothing*. And do you know why?

RUTH: No.

(Pause.)

NICK: You have no self-respect.

RUTH: I don't.

NICK: No.

(Pause.)

RUTH: And then I'm not worth anything. *(Pause.)* So that
when you get—I don't know—when you become
bored, I am supposed to pack up and go off.
To not upset you.
I am supposed to go and drown myself.
And if I don't, I've got no self-respect.

(Pause.)

NICK: That's right.

(RUTH goes to oar, takes it and swings it viciously at him.)

RUTH: I hope you die.

*(He parries the blow and hits her in the mouth. She falls off
the porch. Pause.)*

You don't like women.

NICK: Are you alright?

RUTH: You do not respect me.

(Pause.)

NICK: Are you alright?

RUTH: I don't think that you like women.

NICK: Are you alright? *(Pause.)* I'm sorry.

RUTH: You do not respect me at all.

NICK: Did I hurt you?

RUTH: I don't know . . .

*(*NICK *goes to her.)*

RUTH: Please. Please don't touch me. I am going home.
This is wet. This is all wet.
I'm going home.

NICK: Let me come and dry you off.

RUTH: No. I'm alright. I'm alright here.

(Pause.)

NICK: Did I hurt you?

RUTH: No.

NICK: Good.

(Pause.)

RUTH *(to self):* Oh, who can know what I should do here?

(Pause.)

NICK: Ruth, what did I do to you?

RUTH *(to self)*: Ruth.

NICK: Did I hurt you?

RUTH *(to self)*: This is all wet.

NICK: I got nuts.

RUTH: We look back, we look back at things. The things that we knew. About each other.

NICK: Come in.

RUTH: All those things we knew.

NICK: You're going to catch your death.

RUTH: The Lake. Those things live down there.

NICK: What things?

RUTH: The Plankton.

NICK: Aren't you wet?

RUTH: The screaming.

NICK: Come up.

RUTH: Blood. Your tongue. *(Pause.)* When I had you in me the first time. *(Pause.)* When you had me. *(Pause.)* Must I be *punished? (She starts to cry.)*

NICK: Things change. Oh, this is no good.

RUTH: That's why I wanted to *come* here.
    To get back to Nature.
    We can't do that in the City. *(Pause.)*
    But we could do that *here.*
    You said you loved me.

NICK: When?

RUTH: That time.

NICK: When?

RUTH: You remember.

NICK: No.

RUTH: You do.

NICK: I don't remember.

RUTH: Yes, you do.
    I wouldn't lie about that.

    (Pause.)

NICK: I don't remember.

RUTH: Yes. You told me.

    (Pause.)

NICK: When? *When?*

RUTH: And we watched the lightning.

    (Pause.)

    I guess you're always better off to be the other one.
    She said that when the Polack knifed him, all the clocks
    stopped. On her locket.
    The grandfather clock. They would not tell the time.
    (Pause.) Jacky Weiss said that was just a pile of shit.
    He hit him with a pitchfork in the chest.
    She loved him, though. She always loved him. (Pause.)
    I think my shoulder hurts.

NICK: You want me to put something on it?

RUTH: No.

NICK: A bandage. *(Pause.)* Mercurochrome?

RUTH: Mercurochrome is only water.

NICK: Iodine? Some iodine?

(RUTH *starts to cry.*)

RUTH *(to self):* This *mud* . . .

NICK: I'm sorry, Ruth.

RUTH: Yeah. We will hang on to each other.
    You don't want to know.
    That's why you're stupid.
    "Fuck me, I don't want to die."
    *No*body wants to die.

NICK: I always loved your body.

RUTH: . . . only madmen.
    Sorry, lunatics.
    Oh, yeah, yeah, yeah. Oh, Christ.
    You don't know anything.
    You only hurt yourself.
    Your *own* self.

(Pause.)

NICK: I'm sorry that I hurt you.

RUTH: No. You are a ghoul.
    You never know what's going on.

NICK: I'm sorry, Ruth.

RUTH: I'm *bleeding!*
  Why do you do this? *(Pause.)* That you want to kill me.
  Do you know? *(Pause.)* Do you know? *(She goes over and
  grabs him, and shakes him.)*

NICK: I hit you.

RUTH: Why? *Why?*

NICK: I was frightened.

RUTH: Of what? Tell me. I am not a *witch.* I do not *know.*
  You have to *tell* me. *Why?*

NICK: I thought.

RUTH: What?

NICK: All my life.

RUTH: What?

NICK: All my life I thought that I would *meet* a person.
  She . . .

RUTH: What?

NICK: She would say, "Let us be lovers." *(Pause.)*
  She'd ask me.
  "I know who you are." *(Pause.)*
  "I know you."
  "I know what you need."
  "I want to have your children." *(Pause.)*
  "I understand you."
  "I know what you are."

RUTH *(to self, very softly):* Oh, God.

NICK: I would fall down. I would fall down and thank God.
  I'd thank God for my life.
  I'd kiss the Earth.

RUTH: You read too many books.

NICK: We'd sit here in the Winter and we'd talk and watch
the snow.
And we would think things.

RUTH *(to self):* We could have sat here.

NICK: And I feel these things.

RUTH *(to self):* . . . we could have.

NICK: They confuse me.

(Pause.)

RUTH: Yes. *(She starts to go in.)*

NICK: Where are you going?

RUTH: Well, I have to change my clothes. I'm wet.

NICK: It all gets cold so fast. What is the point?

RUTH: Will you get dressed—because you have to drive
me to the bus?

NICK: No. You should stay with me.

RUTH: No. I cannot. I have to go.

NICK: What is the point? No.
No. What is the point? If one is like the other?

(Pause.)

Where is your friendship in that?

(Pause.)

You made the bracelet. It says you will always love me.
(Pause.) You had it made.
No. You don't have to go.
I don't believe that.

(Pause.)

Why do you have to go?

RUTH: You do not love me.

NICK: How do you know?

RUTH: Nicky . . .

NICK: No. Please. No. Please stay with me.

RUTH: I wish I could.

NICK: But no. You can. You must stay.
      I can't sleep alone, you know that.
      I can't sleep when I am by myself. I have these dreams
      . . . you know that . . .

RUTH: Nick . . .

NICK: I don't feel good.
      I am inside this hole.

RUTH: Come back inside.

NICK: No.

RUTH: Yes. Before it starts to rain.

NICK: Stay with me.

RUTH: No.

NICK: I sit here. Wait. I sit here. It gets dark. I cannot read.
      I need you to be up here. *(Pause.)* I need time. Do you

hear me? I need time. Down in the City everything is vicious. I need time to be up here. *(Pause.)* Everything is filthy down there. *You* know that. I come up here, I see things. *(Pause.)* I cannot sleep. I have these dreams at night. I dream. No, wait. I'll tell you. *(Pause.)* I see the window, and the shades are blowing. There has come a breeze, and all the curtains blow.
They are on fire.
It laps around the window. On all sides.
Someone is calling my name. Nicholas.
I swear to you.
I hear them in a voice unlike a man or woman. When I look, I do not want to know. I know that there is something there. I look. I see a bear. A bear has come back. At the window. Do you hear me, Ruth?
Do you know what this *is?* To crawl beneath my house. This house is *mine* now. In its hole it calls me.
In the Earth. *(Pause.)* Nicholas.
He's standing upright. On his legs. He has a huge erection. I am singed. He speaks a human language, Ruth. I know. He has these thoughts and they are trapped inside his mouth. His jaw cannot move. He has thoughts and feelings, BUT HE CANNOT SPEAK.
If only he could *speak.*
If only he could say the thing he wants.

RUTH: What does he want?

NICK: I DO NOT KNOW!

RUTH: No! *(She hits him.)*

(Pause.)

NICK: It smells like fish up here.

(She hits him again.)

RUTH: You speak to me.

NICK: You know I cannot speak.
    I'm falling.

RUTH: No.

NICK: I'm falling in a hole.

RUTH: There is no hole.

NICK: There is. I do not like the way it smells.

RUTH: You stop this.

NICK: I have seen it all come back.

RUTH: You stop this.

NICK: I don't want to die. Oh, God. I do not want to die.
    I am insane. Am I insane? I knocked you off the porch.
    I hurt you. *(Pause.)* I feel like things are swimming.
    Ruth. Am I insane?

RUTH: No.

NICK: Yes. I am. How can I live like this? I tried to kill you.

RUTH: No. You didn't

NICK: Yes. You know I wanted to. I can't control myself.
    I'm going swimming. *(He starts off the porch.)*

RUTH: Sit down.

NICK: No. I'm going in the water.

RUTH: You sit down.

NICK: I cannot live like this. I'm sorry.

RUTH: You aren't going anywhere. There's nothing wrong
  with you.

NICK: There is.

  (RUTH *hits him.*)

RUTH: You *shit.* You stupid *shit.* You sit down and don't
  move. You are *alright.* You are alright. *(She hits him
  again.)*
  Can't you *hear* me?
  Are you *deaf?*
  You are alright. There's nothing wrong with you.

NICK: I'm going under. *(He starts to get up.)*

RUTH: No. You are not. *(She stops him.)*

NICK: Oh, yes. *(Screaming:)* What are we *doing* here?
  What are we *doing* here?

  (Pause.)

  What will *happen* to us? *We* can't know ourselves.
  . . . How can we *know* ourselves?
  I have to leave.

RUTH: You stop this. I will kill you before you will leave
  this porch alive.

NICK: I'm going under. *(He starts to go.)*

RUTH: No. I *will. (Attacking him:)* I *will.* You *stop!* *(She hits
  him in the face several times. Softer:)* You stop.

  (Pause. He is subdued. They both are on the floor.)

Nicky.

(A long pause.)

NICK: My face hurts.

RUTH: You are just afraid.

(Pause.)

NICK: No.

RUTH: You are alright.

NICK: I don't think that I am.

RUTH: I swear to you. You listen to me.
I swear on my life. You are alright now.

(Pause.)

RUTH: You are alright.

NICK: Hold on to me.

RUTH: Yes. *(She does so.)*

NICK: I feel strange.

RUTH: Yes. Tell me. Tell me.

NICK: Wait. I have to talk to you. I have to tell you something. Wait.

(Pause.)

We would come up here . . .

(Pause.)

I have to tell you we would come up here as children.
(Pause.) Although some things would happen.

RUTH: Yes. Yes.

NICK: But they were alright.

RUTH *(to self):* In the end.

(Pause.)

NICK: Although we were frightened.

RUTH: Yes.

NICK: And many times we'd come up with a friend.
With friends. We'd ask them here. *(Pause.)*
Because we wanted to be with them.
(Pause.) Because . . . *(Pause.)* Wait.
Because we loved them.

RUTH: I know.

(Pause.)

NICK: Oh, my God. *(Pause. He starts to cry.)*
I love you, Ruth.

(Pause.)

RUTH: No.

NICK: I do, I love you, Ruth.

(Pause.)

RUTH: Thank you.

(*Pause.*)

NICK: I love you.

RUTH: No.

NICK: Yes. (*Pause.*)
    Oh, God, I'm tired.

RUTH: I know.

NICK: Can you stay with me?

RUTH: Come here.
    Shhhh.

NICK: Can you stay with me?

RUTH: It's going to be alright.

NICK: Please talk to me.

RUTH: It's going to be alright.

NICK (*pause*): Will you talk to me?

RUTH: What shall I say?

NICK: Just talk to me.
    I think I'm going to go to sleep.

RUTH: You go to sleep now.

NICK: Yes. I have to hear your voice.

RUTH: Alright.

NICK: I am so sleepy.

RUTH: Shhhh. (*Pause.*)
    Shhhh.
    There were two children . . .

Go to sleep. It's alright.
Go to sleep now.
They went for a walk.
Into the Forest. *(Pause.)*
Their Granma told them not to go too far.
Or else they might get lost.
For you must all be careful when you go into the woods.
And they went in.
It started to get dark.
He said he thought that they had lost their way.

NICK: Are you alright?

RUTH: Yes.

NICK: Are you cold?

RUTH: No.
They lay down.

(Pause.)

He put his arms around her.

(Pause.)

They lay down in the Forest and they put their arms around each other.
In the dark. And fell asleep.

(Pause.)

NICK: Go on.

(Pause.)

RUTH: What?

NICK: Go on.

RUTH *(to self):* Go on. . .

NICK: Yes.

(Pause.)

RUTH: The next day . . .

(The lights fade.)

LAKEBOAT

*This Play is Dedicated
to John Dillon
and to Larry Shue.*

Lakeboat was first staged by the Theatre Workshop at Marlboro College, Marlboro, Vermont, in 1970. It then sat in my trunk until John Dillon, Artistic Director of the Milwaukee Rep, discovered it in 1979.

John worked with me on the script, paring, arranging, and buttressing; and its present form is, in large part, thanks to him. I would also like to thank him and the men and women of the Milwaukee Rep—actors, designers, and crew—for their beautiful production of the play.

Lakeboat was first produced by the Court Street Theater, a project of the Milwaukee Repertory Theater, Milwaukee, Wisconsin, April 24, 1980, with the following cast:

PIERMAN	Gregory Leach
DALE	Thomas Hewitt
FIREMAN	Paul Meacham
STAN	Eugene J. Anthony
JOE	Larry Shue
COLLINS	John P. Connolly
SKIPPY	Robert Clites
FRED	Victor Raider-Wexler

This production was directed by John Dillon; settings by Laura Maurer; lighting by Rachel Budin, costumes by Colleen Muscha; properties by Sandy Struth; stage manager, Marcia Orbison.

Scenes:

Characters:

PIERMAN	30s or 40s.
DALE	Ordinary Seaman. 20.
FIREMAN	Engine. 60s.
STAN	Able-Bodied Seaman. Deck. 40s.
JOE	Able-Bodied Seaman. Deck. 40 or 50s.
COLLINS	Second Mate. 30s or 40s.
SKIPPY	First Mate. Late 50s.
FRED	Able-Bodied Seaman. Deck. 30s or 40s.

Setting:

The Lakeboat *T. Harrison.* The engine room, the galley, the fantail (the farthest aft part of the ship), the boat deck, the rail.

The set, I think, should be a *construction* of a Lakeboat, so that all playing areas can be seen at once, no scenery needs to be shifted, and the actors can simply walk from one area to the next as their scenes require.

Scene 1

What Do You Do with a Drunken Sailor?

The Lakeboat is being offloaded. DALE *talks with the* PIERMAN, *who is supervising the offloading.*

PIERMAN: Did you hear about Skippy and the new kid?

DALE: What new kid?

PIERMAN: Night cook. Whatsisname that got mugged?

DALE: No. What happened?

PIERMAN: Well, you know, this new kid is on the beach . . .

DALE: Yeah. . . .

PIERMAN: And, how it happened, he's in East Chicago after the last pay draw . . .

DALE: Yeah. . . .

PIERMAN: . . . last week and drawed all he could and he's making the bars with a C or so in his pocket and flashing the wad every chance he gets. . . .

DALE: Oh boy.

PIERMAN: What does the kid know? What do they know at that age, no offense.

DALE: Yeah.

PIERMAN: And, as I understand it, this slut comes on to him, and they leave the bar and he gets rolled.

DALE: By the whore?

PIERMAN: Yeah, I mean he'd had a few . . .

DALE: The bitch.

PIERMAN: . . . and wasn't in any shape. Anyway she takes his wad and his Z card.

DALE: Not his Z card?

PIERMAN: Yep and his gate pass. . . .

DALE: And he didn't even get laid . . . did he?

PIERMAN: Fuck no, she rolled him first. Then she left.

DALE: Bitch.

PIERMAN: So, he stumbles back to the gate, drunk and sobbing. . . .

DALE: Nothing to be ashamed of. . . .

PIERMAN: The guards won't let him in! I mean he's bleeding, he's dirty. . . .

DALE: You didn't tell me he was bleeding.

PIERMAN: It was understood. . . .

DALE: So, go on.

PIERMAN: And dirty, and no identification. So, of course, they won't let him in.

DALE: Bastards.

PIERMAN: Yeah, well, they're just doing their job.

DALE: I suppose you're right.

PIERMAN: Pretty nice guys, actually.

DALE: I suppose.

PIERMAN: And so . . . where was I?

DALE: The part where they won't let him in.

PIERMAN: And so the guards won't let him in. But, uh
. . . whatsisname, guy about thirty, so, you know him?

DALE: I'm new.

PIERMAN: Well, whatsisname happens to be coming
through and of course he recognizes . . . whatsisname.

DALE: Yeah.

PIERMAN: So, "What happened? Are you alright?"
. . . all that shit. And the guard explains to him how
they can't let the guy through and the guy vouches
right up for him.

DALE: He's a good man, huh?

PIERMAN: And they *still* won't let him through.

DALE: Yeah.

PIERMAN: So, how he got *in* . . .

DALE: Yeah.

PIERMAN: He waited until these guards are looking the
other way . . .

DALE: Yeah.

PIERMAN: . . . at a secretary or a train, I don't know. And they walked right through the main gate.

DALE: Bunch of assholes, huh?

PIERMAN: Well, I don't know. . . . So, what happened with Skippy . . . you know Skippy?

DALE: No.

PIERMAN: The First Mate.

(Pause.)

DALE: Oh yeah.

PIERMAN: So what happened with him is this: The poor slob gets back to the fucking boat—drunk and bleeding and broke, right?

DALE: Poor sonofabitch.

PIERMAN: He gets to the gangway and the second is on deck supervising offloading.

DALE: Right.

PIERMAN: Talking on the box with Skippy, the First Mate, who is up in the bridge. Now, Skippy sees this poor thing tromping up the pier and he says to Collins, the Second, "Collins, we got passengers this trip," which they did, "Get that man below and tell him to stay there until he's sober."

DALE: Huh.

PIERMAN: Although he is a hell of a nice guy, Skippy. Oldest First Mate on the Lakes. Did you know that?

DALE: No.

PIERMAN: Was a Master once. I don't know who for. That's why they call him Skippy.

DALE: How do you know that?

PIERMAN: I heard it. I don't actually know it. But that's why they call him Skippy. And so, anyway, Collins collars the slob and tells him to get below. "Who says so?" the guy says. "The First says so," Collins says. Guigliani, Guilini, something like that.

DALE: What?

PIERMAN: The guy's name. So anyway. Guigliani, whatsisname, says, "Tell the First to go fuck himself."

DALE: Oh, Christ.

PIERMAN: So, as God would have it, at that precise moment the box rings and it's Skippy wanting to talk to Collins. "Collins," he says, "What's holding up the Number Three Hold?" "I'm talking to Guliami," says Collins. "What the all-fired fuck does he have to say that is so important?" says Skippy. "He's telling me I should tell you to go fuck yourself. . . ." says Collins. So Skippy, who bandied enough words at this point, says, "Collins, throw that man in the canal and get Three Hold the fuck offloaded," which I was working on, too, at that point.

DALE: So?

PIERMAN: So what?

DALE: So did he throw him in the canal?

PIERMAN: I don't know, I was below. I *heard* this.

(*Pause.*)

DALE: And where is the guy now?

PIERMAN: What am I, a mindreader? On the beach somewhere, lost his job. Up in East Chicago, I guess.

DALE: Poor sonofabitch.

PIERMAN: Oh, I don't know.

   (*The* PIERMAN *goes on board the boat.*)

Scene 2

Opening

DALE *talks to the audience.* STAN *is on the boat. The* FIREMAN *comes up the gangplank, followed by* JOE.

DALE *(to audience):* That's the Lakeboat. Built 1938 for Czerwiecki Steel. Christened *Joseph Czerwiecki.* Sold to Harrison Steel, East Chicago, Indiana, 1954, renamed *T. Harrison.* Length overall 615 feet. Depth 321 feet. Keel 586 feet. Beam 60. The floating home of 45 men.

FIREMAN: Guigliani got mugged.

DALE: I'm his replacement. Gross tons 8,225. Capacity in tons 11,406. A fair-sized boat. A small world . . .

FIREMAN: So I've heard.

(JOE *comes on board.*)

STAN: Yo, Joe.

JOE: Hiya.

DALE: . . . *T. Harrison.* A steel bulk-freight turbine steamer registered in the Iron Ore Trade.

STAN: You pick up those razor blades?

JOE: Shit. I fucking forgot, I'm sorry.

Scene 3

Drink

A conversation on the fantail. STAN *and* JOE *are killing time while the boat is at the pier.*

STAN: Boy was I drunk last night.

JOE: I'm still drunk.

STAN: That wine. Drink wine and it dehydrates you. When you drink water the next morning it activates the alcohol.

JOE: I'm so hung over I can't see.

STAN: Can't see, I can't even talk.

JOE: I can't even fucking think straight.

STAN: You couldn't think straight last night.

JOE: I was drunk last night.

STAN: You're still drunk.

JOE: Yep.

STAN: No good, man.

JOE: Yep.

STAN: No damn good.

JOE: Sure not.

STAN: No fucking good.

JOE: What? . . . Drinking?

STAN: Drinking, life, women, the Boat. No good.

JOE: It's not that bad.

STAN: No fuckin' good.

JOE: You been drinking?

STAN: Drinking? Don't talk to me about drinking. What
the hell did it ever get me? Drinking? I was drinking
before you were wiping your own ass. Beer? I've drunk
more beer in my time than I can remember. I could
tick off my life in beer caps. Bottles, cans, pop-tops,
screw-tops, bottles . . . every man on the ship had his
own opener.

JOE: I remember.

STAN: Around the neck. Holy Mary. Don't tell me about
beer, Joe. Please don't tell me about beer. Domestic
and imported. Beer? I've drunk beer. . . . Wine!

JOE: Ah, wine.

STAN: Used to drink it with every meal. White, cherry.
Love the stuff. You need a taste for wine.

JOE: I've got one.

STAN: Domestic and imported.

JOE: I love the stuff.

STAN: Red and *white.* I've drunk it. Wine with my food, cigarettes smoldering and chilled wine. Wine with fruit. Warmed, spice wine. Sweet cherry wine. I know wine, Joe.

JOE: What about liquors?

STAN: What about them?

JOE: Yeah.

STAN: For faggots. But booze . . .

JOE: Booze!

STAN: Scotch and rye. Drink bourbon by the fifth. When I lived at home? Drink? My father could drink.

JOE: My father could, too.

STAN: I say that man could put it *away.* A fifth a day and more, Joe, and *more.*

JOE: My father, too.

STAN: He loved the stuff.

JOE: It killed him, my father.

STAN: Drink it by the fifth. He never lacked for booze, that man. That's one thing I can say for him.

JOE: Yeah.

STAN: Nothing too good for him.

JOE: Yeah.

STAN: The old fart'd drink Sterno. He didn't give a shit.

JOE: I know.

STAN: That man could *drink.*

JOE: What about your mother?

STAN: She could drink, too.

JOE: My mother couldn't drink.

STAN: No?

JOE: Old man said it was bad for her.

STAN: What do they know of booze, the cunts?

JOE: Nothing.

STAN: They can't drink. You ever know a woman who could drink?

JOE: Yeah.

STAN: What do they know?

JOE: A girl in Duluth.

STAN: They don't understand it. It's a man's thing, drinking. A curse and an elevation. Makes you an angel. A booze-ridden angel. Drinking? I know my alcohol, boyo. I know it and you know I know it. And I know it.

JOE: I'll take you below. I gotta go on watch.

STAN: Domestic and imported.

JOE: Come on, Stan.

STAN: Any way you call it.

JOE: I gotta go on watch.

STAN: Mixed drinks? I know my mixed drinks. You name one, I know it. Mixed drinks.

JOE: . . . Manhattan.

STAN: I know it.

JOE: Come on, Stan.

STAN: Ah, leave me alone.

JOE: Come on, I gotta go on watch.

STAN: So go on watch, you fucking Polack.

JOE: Who's a Polack?

STAN: Trust a Polack . . . to go on watch . . . when I'm pissed.

JOE: I'll take you down to the dunnage room and get you some coffee.

STAN: Don't want any coffee. Want to go to sleep.

JOE: Well, let's go, then.

STAN: I want to sleep by myself.

JOE: Okay, Stan, let's get you off your feet.

STAN: Offa deck.

JOE: Sure.

STAN: And who are you to tell me to get off the deck of a ship we both happen to be on?

JOE: Come on, goddamnit.

STAN: Getting mad, huh?

JOE: Stosh.

STAN: Getting a trifle warm. Aren't you getting warm?

JOE: Okay, Stan.

STAN: Fucking no-class Polack.

JOE: Okay, Stan.

STAN: Can't even hold your liquor.

(JOE *walks off.*)

Scene 4

Offloading

JOE *wanders into the galley.* COLLINS *finds him there and puts him to work.*

COLLINS: Litko!

JOE: Yo!

COLLINS: Skippy wants a sandwich.

JOE: . . . I just came on.

COLLINS: Get him a sandwich, will you?

JOE: I just came *on.* . . .

COLLINS: It'll take you a minute.

JOE: Uh.

COLLINS: *Huh?*

JOE: What about the nightman?

COLLINS: He got mugged.

JOE: Yeah? By who?

COLLINS: Now, how the fuck should I know?

JOE: You got a cigarette?

   (Pause.)

COLLINS: Yeah.

JOE: Thanks.

   (PIERMAN enters galley.)

PIERMAN: Hot.

COLLINS: Can we speed this up at all?

PIERMAN: You'll be out by about two.

COLLINS: You think?

PIERMAN: Two, three. Got time for a cup?

COLLINS: Yeah. Joe, go see what kind of sandwich Skippy wants, huh?

JOE: Yeah. *(Exits.)*

PIERMAN: Any chance of something to eat?

COLLINS: Lost the nightman.

PIERMAN: Oh yeah. . . . Sorry.

COLLINS *(pause):* Cook's up the street. *(Pause.)* You want some pie?

PIERMAN: Yeah.

COLLINS: Any special kind?

PIERMAN: Yeah, blueberry. What you got?

COLLINS: We got some.

PIERMAN: It's a bitch in here.

COLLINS: Yeah.

PIERMAN: Cooler on the dock.

COLLINS: Yeah.

PIERMAN: What's the next trip, Arthur?

COLLINS: Duluth.

PIERMAN: Yeah? Cool up there.

(JOE *enters.*)

COLLINS *(to* JOE*):* What'd he want?

JOE: Egg on white bread.

PIERMAN: Any guys on break out there, you notice?

JOE: I didn't notice.

PIERMAN: Uh.

JOE: I was thinking about my sandwich. We gonna have a new nightman, Mr. Collins?

COLLINS: Huh?

JOE: Nightman.

COLLINS: Yeah, sure. Crender said we'll have him this trip.

JOE: That's good. I don't want to make these sandwiches all the way to Canada. If you know what I mean. Not that I mind it. I just fucking hate making sandwiches. For other people to eat.

COLLINS: Don't worry.

JOE: I don't mind cooking for myself, though.

COLLINS: Wrap it in wax paper, will you?

JOE: Yeah, sure.

COLLINS *(leaving the galley):* And make sure you get those boats clean today, huh?

JOE: Right as rain.

Scene 5

Fire and Evacuation Drills

SKIPPY, *making a tour of the boat, runs into* DALE.

SKIPPY: That's right, assholes. Fuck off on your fire and evacuation drills and your ass is going to be in a big sling when we have to drill for the Coast Guard. You!

DALE: Yes sir.

SKIPPY: What's your number?

DALE: What number, sir?

SKIPPY: F and E. *(Pause.)* F and E, boy—

DALE: I don't know what that means, sir.

SKIPPY: Fire. Fire and evacuation.

DALE: I . . . don't think I have one.

SKIPPY: How long have you been on this ship?

DALE: About three minutes, sir.

SKIPPY: Yeah. Well, check out your fire and evacuation number, for God's sake, will you? Your F and E number, will you?

DALE: Yessir. Who do I check it out with?

SKIPPY: I do not know. Ask Joe Litko. You know him?

DALE: I can find him, sir.

SKIPPY: Good for you. Well, find him and listen hard.

DALE: Yessir.

SKIPPY: Bunch of children.

Scene 6

The Illusion of Motion

SKIPPY *continues back to the bridge, where he finds* COLLINS.

SKIPPY: Where's my sandwich?

COLLINS: Litko's getting it.

SKIPPY: He's not in Stewards. Where's the nightman?

COLLINS: Got mugged. He's in the hospital.

SKIPPY: What's the number in Stewards?

COLLINS: 2—3.

SKIPPY: Call for me on that sandwich.

COLLINS *(on the intercom):* Stewards? Collins calling on that sandwich for Skippy. Well, who is there? Where's Litko? Well, get him.

(Pause.)

This is Collins, Second . . . (to SKIPPY:) they hung up. *(He spies* LITKO *on the deck.)* There's Litko. LITKO! GO PICK UP THE DECK PHONE. NO! DON'T COME HERE, PICK UP THE PHONE.

(STAN and FRED passing by.)

STAN: This boat is becoming a bureaucracy.

FRED: Tell me. *(They continue off. Phone rings.)*

COLLINS *(into phone):* Bridge, Collins. Litko, I've been try-
    ing to get you. What the fuck happened on Skippy's
    egg? Where have you been? Boatdeck? What about
    that sandwich. *(To SKIPPY:)* New nightman showed up.

SKIPPY: Book him. Forget Litko.

COLLINS *(into phone):* Litko, forget it. Go back to the boats.
    Yeah. No. Forget it. *(He hangs up.)*

SKIPPY: What's he doing on the boatdeck?

COLLINS: Reading.

SKIPPY: What's he reading? See if you can find out.

(STAN and FRED stroll off.)

STAN *(to FRED):* Who was the most grotesque girl you ever
    fucked?

FRED: I'd have to think about that.

SKIPPY: I'd like to know.

Scene 7

The New Man

COLLINS *returns to the galley and encounters* DALE.

COLLINS: You the new man?

DALE: I guess.

COLLINS: You're going to be the new nightman. Night-
cook. You ever cooked before?

DALE: No, a little.

COLLINS: Well, we're going to book you nightman, what's
your name?

DALE: Katzman, Dale.

COLLINS: Alright. We're going to book you. Then you're
off until 10 P.M. tonight. You work ten till six-thirty
straight shift. Half-hour for lunch. Your work should
take you about four, five hours.

(Phone rings.)

Get that.

DALE: Hello, kitchen. Wait a minute. He wants the Mate.

COLLINS: Gimme that. Collins. Yo. They're off. He got mugged. We got one. What kind? Fuck you. Okay. *(To* DALE:*)* You know how to make a sandwich?

DALE: Sure.

COLLINS: Make one for the First. The First Mate. And then make one for the Fireman.

DALE: Right. What kind?

COLLINS: For the First, an egg . . . and for the Fireman, how the fuck should I know? Make him an egg. Alright?

DALE: Sure.

COLLINS: Good.

Scene 8

Woploving

The FIREMAN, JOE, *and* STAN *are shooting the breeze in the engine room.*

FIREMAN: So, the way I hear it: she told him she was divorced. How about that.

JOE: So what?

FIREMAN: I'm divorced.

JOE: Sorry.

FIREMAN: So they started to get really blind.

JOE: My mother is blind.

(Pause.)

FIREMAN: And could he spare her some change, twenty for the kids, a saw for some groceries, you know.

JOE: Yeah.

FIREMAN: And all of the time she's drinking this rum with coke and lime.

JOE: Coke *and* lime?

FIREMAN: That's what I heard.

JOE: That's how they drink it in Italy.

FIREMAN: You never been to Italy.

JOE: Now how the FUCK do you know?

FIREMAN: I . . .

JOE: How the everlasting cocksucking FUCK do you know
I never been to Italy?

FIREMAN: Jesus.

JOE: Don't do shit all day and tells me where I never been.
(Exits.)

FIREMAN *(to Stan):* So, Collins tells me, she'd have a
drink . . .

STAN: Yeah.

FIREMAN: He'd have a drink.

STAN: Yeah.

FIREMAN: But pretty soon he's getting up knocking over
tables and he's staggering ready to die and she's walk-
ing in a straight line. Say, I wonder what's the matter
with Joe?

STAN: Why do you say something's the matter with him?

FIREMAN: I only . . .

STAN: Who the hell are you?

FIREMAN: I only meant . . .

STAN: Twenty-some years on the boats watching a little
dial and you know about what's "wrong with Joe?"

FIREMAN: Lookit . . .

STAN: Just listen to me. The man has done more shit in his life than you'll ever *forget*.

FIREMAN: I only said . . .

STAN: Just remember that, Mr. Wiseass. He's been more places in his life than you *ever* been.

FIREMAN: He's never been to Italy.

STAN: What kind of woploving bullshit is that?

FIREMAN: *I'm* fucking Italian, don't talk to *me*, Fred.

DALE *(enters the engine room; generally):* Hi.

STAN: Hi.

(Pause.)

Dale: How are you?

STAN: Fine.

DALE: That's good.

STAN: In the sense that I feel like shit. Been to Italy. *(He exits.)*

DALE: You want a sandwich?

FIREMAN: Yeah. You the new nightman?

DALE: Yes. Do you like egg?

FIREMAN: I don't give a fuck.

Scene 9

Gauges

DALE: What do you do down here?

FIREMAN: Down here? I read.

DALE: How can you read and do your job?

FIREMAN: I'm not answerable to you. I'm answerable to the Chief.

DALE: I was just asking.

FIREMAN: I do my job okay.

DALE: I know that.

FIREMAN: I do it okay. I keep busy. . . . I read a bit. . . .

DALE: It doesn't get in your way, the reading?

FIREMAN: Nooo. I mean, I gotta watch the two gauges. Four actually. We got the two main, they're the two you gotta watch, and the two auxiliary.

DALE: Uh huh.

FIREMAN: But you gotta keep your eye on those two main, because if they go, well . . .

DALE: *Oh,* yeah.

FIREMAN: I mean if that main goes, if she goes redline, you're fucking fucked.

DALE: You switch over to the auxiliary?

FIREMAN: I don't do nothing! I don't do a damn nothing. I'm not supposed to touch a thing. I shut down whichever blows, larboard or starboard. I shut down and I call the bridge and I call in the Chief, in that order.

DALE: And then you watch the auxiliary?

FIREMAN: Nothing to watch. The engine's shut down and the gauges is dead.

DALE: Well, what's the point of having an auxiliary gauge?

FIREMAN: For a standby. You gotta have a standby. . . .

DALE: Oh.

FIREMAN: You don't have a standby, with that automatic oil feed! You don't have a standby and the main goes, you're fucking *fucked.* You know what I mean.

DALE: Oh yeah.

(Pause.)

And you keep an eye on them, huh?

FIREMAN: What do you mean, "keep an eye on them?" I'm watching 'em constantly. That's my job.

DALE: I see that.

FIREMAN: Of course, I read a *bit.* I mean, when you get down to it. What is there to do? Watching two gauges for four hours a clip?

DALE: Uh huh.

FIREMAN: That's eight hours a day watching two gauges. If you don't read, do something, you'd go insane.

Scene 10

No Pussy

DALE *climbs up out of the engine room and is accosted by* FRED.

FRED: You the new man?

DALE: Yep. Dale. Dale Katzman.

FRED: Jewish, huh?

DALE: Yeah.

FRED: No offense.

DALE: Thanks.

   (Pause.)

FRED: Well, Dale . . . Coming on like this out of nowhere you got a thing or two to find out. Now, the main thing about the boats, other than their primary importance in the Steel Industry, is that you don't get any pussy. You got that?

DALE: Yes.

FRED: Except when we tie up. This is important to know because it precludes your whole life on the boats. This is why everyone says "fuck" all the time.

DALE: Why?

FRED: They say "fuck" in direct proportion to how bored they are. Huh?

DALE: Yeah.

FRED: Now, from the prospect of not getting any . . . you know about sex?

DALE: I know it all.

FRED: I see you mean that facetiously.

DALE: Yeah.

FRED: Because there sure is a hell of a lot to find out. I'm not going to offend you, am I?

DALE: I don't know.

FRED: Okay.

(Pause.)

You know, I didn't find out about sex until late in life, judging from my age of puberty, you gotta go on watch?

DALE: Not until ten.

FRED: . . . which came quite early, who can say why? Huh?

DALE: Yeah.

FRED: Around eight. What did I know then, right? Stroke books, jacking off with a few choice friends, you know. Am I right?

DALE: You're right.

FRED: For *years*. Until I'm in high school and I fall for this girl. Same old story, right? She's beautiful, she's smart, and I dig her. I take her out, right? So, times are different then (this was a few years ago) and after the movies we're dryhumping in the living room. The father is asleep upstairs, the mother is dead, same old story, right?

DALE: Right.

FRED: And all of a sudden the whole thing becomes clear to me. I mean in a flash all this horseshit about the Universe becomes clear to me, and I perceive meaning in life: I WANT TO FUCK. I want to stick it inside of her. Screw dryhumping. I want to get it wet. I want to become one with the ages of men and women before me down into eternity and goo in the muck from whence we sprung . . . you know what I mean?

DALE: I know.

FRED: And I'm on fire. I'm going OOOOOOOOOoh and AAAAAAAAAAAaaah and like that and trying to undo her brassiere. (This girl had tits.) I don't even bother anymore. You know what I say? "You do it," I say. The joy is gone, you know? So, anyway. We're
● still humping and bumping and I'm trying to undo the brassiere and my knee, as if it had a mind of its own, and never a word spoken, had inserted itself between her legs and she's gyrating like crazy and saying . . . What do you think she is saying?

DALE: "I love you?"

FRED: "No," she is saying, "Oh, Fred, please don't."

DALE: So?

FRED: So, like a dope, I don't. We look sheepish for a minute. She gets all straightened out and says she had a wonderful time, Freddy, and out I go. So, to make a long story short, after this happened another time, two times, I begin to get wise something is not as it should be. Also, I can't walk in the mornings. But my uncle, who is over, is conversing with me one night and, as men will do, we start talking about sex. He tells a story, I tell *my* story. This takes him aback. "What?" he says. "The way to get laid is to treat them like shit." Now, you just stop for a moment and think on that. You've heard it before and you'll hear it again but there is more to it than meets the eye. Listen: THE WAY TO GET LAID IS TO TREAT THEM LIKE SHIT. Truer words have never been spoken. And this has been tested by better men than you or me. *So,* I thought it out a bit and decided to put it into action. I'm going out with Janice. Movies, walk home, couch, dryhumping, no . . . I hit her in the mouth. I don't mean slap, Dale, this is important. I mean hit, I fucking pasted her. She didn't know nothing. She is so surprised she didn't even bleed. Not a word did I speak, but off with her dress, panties, and my pants. I didn't wear any underwear. A lot of women find that attractive, did you know that?

DALE: No.

FRED: Well, I've only since found that out. Anyway. Smacko, spread the old chops and I humped the shit out of her. She's yelling: OOOOh. Don't, OOOOH, yessssssssss, OOOOooooh don't, Freddy, Yes, it's so gooooooooood, my father'll hear oooooooh. SHEEEEEEEEEEEEIT. Zingo. So I got dressed and she's lying there on the couch spent, I mean, spent and wet and everything. (She looked beautiful.) And I go over to the door. "Not another word out of you, cunt," I say. "Ever."

DALE: What about her father?

FRED: He was a boilermaker. So. After that it's handjobs in the assembly hall, fucking under the bleachers, the whole thing, man. She's buying presents and asking *me* to the prom (I'd left school). And to this day. I mean to this day, I want a piece, I call her up and tell her, not ask her, *tell* Daley, I tell her where and when, and she's there. And she's *married.* So remember. . . . I know, I *know,* I was a shy kid *too.* But you gotta remember, the way to a woman's cunt is right through her cunt. That's the only way. *Fershtay?*

DALE: Uh huh.

FRED: Let's get something to eat.

DALE: I gotta make up the First's cabin.

FRED: Okay. I'm gonna see you later.

(JOE *and* STAN *pass. Part of their conversation can be heard.*)

JOE: Guy can't take care of himself he oughta stay out of East Chicago. *Huh?*

STAN: Yeah.

(*Pause.*)

JOE: They aren't in business for their health. . . .

Scene 11

Mugged

FRED, *alone by the rail, soliloquizes.*

FRED: Mugged. Yeah. Poor son of bitch. In East Chicago. That's a lousy town. By some whore, no less. Drugged the shit out of him, I guess. Met her in a bar. Who knows. He was a fanatic, you know? I knew him. Not overly well, but I knew him. He was a gambling degenerate. Played the ponies. How did he do I don't know. But I had my suspicions that he gave it all away. So who knows. Maybe the Maf got him. I mean, somebody got him. Maybe the whore, huh? So maybe it's the Murphy man, but I don't think so. It looks like the Outfit. Not that they care for the few C's they took. But you know how they are. You can't get behind. When you're into them that's it. Am I right? No. It doesn't figure. Unless it was the Outfit. Or some freak occurrence. It was probably some Outfit guys got him. Assuming he was into them. It doesn't look like he just got rolled. Beat the living fuck out of him. Left him for dead. Huh? Can you feature it? Flies in his face. Fucking ear stuck to the sidewalk with blood. Ruptured

man, he'll never perform again. Ribs, back. The *back.*
Hit him in the back. Left him for *dead.*

(Pause.)

It doesn't figure. The only way it adds up, if it was the
Outfit. A very property-oriented group. Poor sucker.

Scene 12

Fred Busted at the Track

FRED *wanders into the galley, where he meets* STAN.

STAN: Boy, did I get laid last night.

FRED: One of the guys on the boat?

STAN: By a woman, Freddie, a woman. You remember them? Soft things with a hole in the middle.

FRED: I remember them.

STAN: You look down, Freddy.

FRED: I am down.

(*Pause.*)

Why did they have to go and build a racetrack on the south side of Chicago?

STAN: Somebody made a survey. What did you lose?

FRED: Seven hundred bucks.

STAN: Where'd you get seven hundred bucks?

FRED: Around.

STAN: Oh.

(Pause.)

You in trouble?

FRED: No.

STAN: You sure?

FRED: Yeah.

(Pause.)

STAN: You sure?

FRED: Yeah. Thank you. Yeah.

STAN: You'd tell me if you were?

FRED: Yeah.

(Pause.)

STAN: Okay you watch yourself. (He leaves the galley.)

FRED: Thank you.

Scene 13

Fred on Horseracing

FRED *continues his soliloquy.*

FRED: Because it's clean. The track is clean. It's like life without all the complicating people. At the track there are no two ways. There is win, place, show, and out-of-the-money. You decide, you're set. I mean, how clean can you get? Your bet is down and it's DOWN. And the winners always pay. Something. Into the turn, backstretch, spinning into the turn and heading for home. It's poetry. It's a computer. You don't even have to look at the fucking things. It's up on the board and it's final and there are two types of people in the world.

(Pause.)

Next post in fifteen minutes.

COLLINS *(entering the galley):* The next post is up your ass if you don't get to work.

FRED: I'm gone.

(FRED leaves the galley and runs into JOE on the deck.)

JOE: *(as if resuming a conversation):* . . . why I never got along with women. I just had too much dynamite in me.

FRED: . . . it happens. . . .

(They walk down the fantail.)

Scene 14

Personal Sidearms

SKIPPY *and* COLLINS *are on the bridge.*

SKIPPY: . . . the *Luger* was the enlisted man's sidearm, and the *Walther* was the officer's.

COLLINS: Are you sure?

SKIPPY: I was *there,* my friend. I was *there.* . . .

Scene 15

The Cook Story

JOE *and* FRED *on the fantail.*

FRED: I heard the cook has two Cadillac Eldorados.

JOE: This year's?

FRED: Last year. One in Chicago, Chicago Harbor, and the other in Arthur.

JOE: How long's he been on the run?

FRED: About twenty years, I guess.

JOE: Yeah.

FRED: More or less . . . ten, twenty years.

JOE: What's he want with two Caddies?

FRED: So's he can have one here and one there.

JOE: So he can have one everywhere he goes.

FRED: Yeah. Well, he's only got two. He's not married.

JOE: That's it. That's the big difference. Right?

FRED: You said it. That's the difference . . . between him . . .

JOE: Yeah, that's it. Cocksucker can probably *afford* two cars.

FRED: Oh, yeah. Well, he's got 'em.

JOE: Cocksucker probably doesn't know what it *is* to be married.

FRED: He was married once.

JOE: Yeah?

FRED: Yeah, I think. Yeah. He was married. I heard that.

JOE: Where'd you hear it, on the Boat?

FRED: Yeah. He used to be married. To a girl. She used to ship on the Boats.

JOE: Yeah?

FRED: Oh yeah, they used to ship Stewards together. They stopped. They got divorced.

JOE: Bastard's probably forgot what it is to be married.

(Pause.)

Two cars.

FRED: What the fuck? He worked for them.

JOE: I'm not saying he didn't work for them.

FRED: Oh no.

JOE: I never said that, I mean, it's obvious he worked for them. He's got 'em, right?

FRED: As far as I know.

JOE: Well, has he got 'em or not?

FRED: Yeah, he's got 'em . . . as far as I know.

JOE: Probably only got a couple of Chevys.

FRED: Yeah.

JOE: A couple of '56 Chevys.

FRED: Yeah.

JOE: Cocksucker's only probably got a pair of used Volks-
wagens.

FRED: I don't know. . . .

JOE: Or a beat-up Buick.

FRED: Yeah.

JOE: Or a fucking De*Soto* for Christ's sake. Who the fuck
knows he's got two Caddies?

FRED: Well, he's not married. I know that much.

JOE: Lucky son of a bitch.

FRED: It's a tough life.

JOE: Oh yeah?

FRED: Yeah. I was married once.

JOE: Yeah?

FRED: Yeah. I'm still married. To my second wife.

JOE: You got divorced, huh?

FRED: Why do you say that?

JOE: You just said you're married to your second wife.

FRED: Oh yeah. I got divorced . . . from my first.

Joe: Yeah, I'm sorry. I mean, she could of died. You could of been a widower.

Fred: It's too late now.

Joe: You pay any alimony?

Fred: Yeah, ho, shit, did I pay? I was doing extra deck-work and running to the track so that woman could fuck off and pamper the kids.

Joe: How many kids you have?

Fred: . . . just one, actually. I don't know why I said "kids."

Joe: They live with their mother, huh?

Fred: Yeah. Actually there's just one kid, Clarice. She's the kid.

Joe: A girl, huh?

Fred: Yeah. She lives with her mother.

Joe: You see her?

Fred: Oh yeah. What do you think? I just let her live with that cunt? Christ. I see her every chance I get. Her birthday . . . we go to the *zoo* . . . museums. . . . She got married, my wife, ex.

Joe: Well, shit. At least you don't have to pay alimony.

Fred: Yeah. But doesn't she fuck me on the child support? Every fucking piece of kleenex has to come from Carson Pirie Scott. What fucking kid spends eighty dollars a month? What happens to eighty dollars a month? I'll tell you, Denise ex-fucking-Swoboda is what happens. Nothing is too good for the kid. But it takes a bite.

Joe: What doesn't?

FRED: That is a point, Joe. It's getting expensive just to
  live.

JOE: Sure as shit.

FRED: Just to buy a pack of Camels is getting you have to
  go to the fucking bank. Used to be twenty-six cents a
  pack in Indiana.

JOE: I can remember it used to be seventeen cents in
  Tennessee.

FRED: You aren't from there.

JOE: We used to go there.

FRED: Ah.

JOE *(pause):* I wish I never got started. I used to buy 'em
  for my old man. He used to say, "You gotta smoke,
  don't hide it. Smoke in my presence."

FRED: So did you?

JOE: Christ no, he woulda beat the shit outta me.

FRED: You should never of gotten started. It's too fucking
  expensive. Fuck. Eighty-five cents.

JOE: It's going up.

FRED: Where is it going to stop? I swear to God I don't
  know. We'll all be selling syphilitic fucking apples to
  each other on the street corner.

JOE: You give any money on Poppyseed days?

FRED: No. They want loot, let 'em work on the ship.

JOE: I always wanted to be a pirate. Ever since I was a little
  kid.

FRED: . . . or digging ditches, though somebody's gotta run the ships, right?

JOE: . . . yeah.

FRED: I mean, the cook's gotta keep up his payments.

JOE: That's a good one, alright.

Scene 16

Sidearms Continued

On the bridge.

COLLINS: So what was the Walther Luger.

SKIPPY: There was no such thing.

COLLINS: I read it.

SKIPPY: Where?

COLLINS: In some book on the War.

SKIPPY: Then you were lied to. There was no such thing. Believe me.

   (Pause.)

COLLINS: I *read* it.

SKIPPY: No. I'd tell you if it were the case. *(Pause.)* I would. If it were the case.

Scene 17

Jonnie Fast

FRED *and* STAN *are smoking cigarettes on the boat deck.*

FRED: I'm going to *tell* you: Jonnie Fast is the strongest guy in ten years.

STAN: You know what? You are truly an idiot. You could of said that in the dark and I would of known it was you because only you could make so stupid a statement. Jonnie Fast has got to be the dumbest cocksucker I can remember.

FRED: Yeah. That's like you to say that.

STAN: You know about it . . . ?

FRED: I know when a guy is strong.

STAN: And that's what Fast is. Strong, huh?

FRED: Yeah.

STAN: You know. I agree with you one hundred percent. He is strong, this Fast. He's probably the strongest guy I've ever seen. I can't think of anything that would be stronger than he is. Unless maybe a pile of shit.

FRED: What do you know. Who do you like?

STAN: Oh . . . I'll tell you. You want a really *strong* fellow. A real type, I'd have to say . . . Jerry Lewis. He could probably knock the shit outta Fast.

FRED: You don't know nothing. You don't know a champ when you're fucking looking at him at the movies, for chrissake. This guy is stark. He is the best.

STAN: He's the best, alright. Like jacking off is better than getting laid. This guy Fast is the fucking jackoff of all time.

FRED: Yeah. I see your point, Stan. I agree with you. The man is not stark. He's no fucking good. That's why he didn't take five fucking guys in that barroom using only one pool cue. I see your point.

STAN: Shirley Temple probably couldn't've taken those guys, I suppose.

FRED: Oh, no. Shirley Temple probably could've taken them. She could've disarmed them and probably shot that meat knife out've the guy's hand from twenty feet from the hip . . . yeah, I see your point.

STAN: And I suppose this guy could whip the shit out've Clint Eastwood, huh? I really think that. Explain that to me, will you, Joe? How Clint Eastwood is no match for this guy?

FRED: Oh, well . . .

STAN: No, explain it to me.

FRED: If you want to get ridiculous about it . . .

STAN: Or Lee Van Cleef. I'm *sure,* he would've laid down and puked from fear when he saw this guy two blocks off.

FRED: All I know is, like you say, any guy who fucks all night and drinks a shitload of champagne and can go out at five the next morning and rob a bank without a hitch has to be no fucking good. I see your point.

STAN: "No fucking good?" No! He's great! He only had the entire National Guard worth of sidekicks, about two thousand guys and an A-bomb to back him up. You really gotta admire a stand-up guy like that.

FRED: He didn't have no bomb.

STAN: Pardon me.

FRED: Where do you get this "bomb" shit? You probably didn't even see the movie, all you know.

STAN: No, you're right. I probably didn't even see the movie. That's how come I don't know what a bustout Jonnie Fast is, and what a complete loser you are to back him. I probably never did see the picture. In fact, I've probably never been to a movie in my life and I'm not standing on a boat. And your name isn't Fred, I suppose. Oh, and you're probably not completely full of shit.

FRED: Probably not.

STAN: You idiot, what do you know.

(STAN walks off.)

Scene 18

The Inland Sea around Us

JOE, *on the boat deck, is contemplating the lake.* COLLINS, *making his evening rounds, walks by.*

JOE: Evening, Mr. Collins.

COLLINS: Joe.

JOE: Mr. Collins, how far is it to land out here?

COLLINS: I don't know, about five miles.

JOE: How long could a guy live out here, do you think?

COLLINS: What?

JOE: I mean, not if he was on an island or anything, or in a boat. I mean in the water. I mean . . . it's over your head.

COLLINS: Don't really know, Joe. You planning a swim?

JOE: Swim? Swim? Oh! I get you. A swim! Yeah, no. I was just wondering in case, God forbid, we should go down and the lifeboats were all leaky or something. How long do you think a fellow would last?

COLLINS: Joe . . .

JOE: You can tell me.

COLLINS: Don't worry about it, huh? Even if the boat sunk you've got jackets and they'd have a helicopter here in a half-hour.

JOE: Oh, I don't worry about it. I just wonder. You know.

COLLINS: Sure, Joe. Well, don't wonder.

JOE: I guess the big problem wouldn't be the drowning as much as the boredom, huh?

COLLINS: See you, Joe.

JOE: Night, Mr. Collins.

Scene 19

Arcana

Stan *and* Joe *walk across the fantail.*

Stan: There are many things in this world, Joe, the true meaning of which we will never know. *(Pause.)* I knew a man was a Mason . . .

Joe: Uh huh . . .

Stan: You know what he told me?

Joe: No.

> *(Pause.)*

Stan: Would you like to know?

Joe: Yes.

> *(As* Stan *starts to speak, they continue around the fantail and out of sight.)*

Scene 20

Dolomite

COLLINS *continues to the bridge.* SKIPPY *is in command of the ship.* COLLINS *philosophizes.*

COLLINS *(to* SKIPPY*):* You know, it's surprising what people will convince themselves is interesting. The Company, guests come on for a trip and we're docked at Port Arthur and they're up on the boatdeck and for an hour, an hour and a half, they're watching this stuff pour into the holds. Just watching it pour into the holds and the dust is flying and it's hard to breathe. But they're just standing there. The woman's got a Brownie. She's taking pictures of rock falling off a conveyor belt. Now what is so interesting about that? I'd like to know. If you described the situation to them, to any normal people, they wouldn't walk across the hall to watch it if the TV were broken. But there they are, guests of the Company. Standing there on the boatdeck hours on end, watching the rocks and the dust. Maybe they see something I don't. Maybe I'm getting jaded.

(Pause.)

What are they looking at?

SKIPPY: What are *you* looking at? You're looking at them.

COLLINS: That's perfectly correct.

SKIPPY: It's all a matter of perspective. *(Pause.) Yes*sir.

(Pause.)

Scene 21

The Bridge

SKIPPY *is alone as* COLLINS *leaves the bridge.* JOE *and* DALE *are alone in the galley.*

SKIPPY *(on the radio):* W.A.Y., Chicago, this is the *T. Harrison,* Harrison Steel, en route. I am ready to copy. Over.

JOE: What time you go off?

DALE: Around six-thirty.

JOE: Hit the bridge before then.

DALE: Yeah.

JOE: Hit it in about a half-hour.

DALE: Yeah.

JOE: Hit it about six. You made up the First's cabin yet?

DALE: Yeah. I was up forward a little while ago. Going to be a nice day.

JOE: Hot.

DALE: You think?

JOE: Yeah. Well, be hot when we tie up. Be hot before we hit the Soo. You going up the street?

DALE: Oh, I don't know. Later maybe. Going to get some sleep first.

JOE: They got some nice bars up there.

DALE: Yeah?

JOE: Oh yeah. I know. Got some real bars up there. Sedate . . . Yeah. I used to go up there. To go drinking up there.

DALE: You off now?

JOE: Naw. I don't go off till the eight o'clock come on. I don't go off till eight.

DALE: You hungry?

JOE: Yeah, a little.

DALE: Want me to fix you something?

JOE: Naw. I'll get me some pie, something. We got any pie left?

DALE: Should be some. Want something to drink? A glass of milk?

JOE: Naw, I'll just get some coffee. You know, Dale . . . you go to school?

DALE: Yeah, I'm in my second year.

JOE: You're starting your second year, you finished one year?

DALE: Yeah. I'll be starting my sophomore year in September. When I go back.

JOE: Where do you go at?

DALE: In Massachusetts. Near Boston.

JOE: What do you go all the way there for?

DALE: Well, I like it there. It's a good school. . . . It's a nice area.

JOE: Yeah, but they got good schools over here, don't they? I mean, I'm sure it's a good place . . . where you go. But they got good schools here, too. Loyola, Chicago University, some good schools here . . . Michigan.

DALE: Oh, yeah. They're good schools. But I like it in the East.

JOE: It's nice there, huh?

DALE: Yes, very nice. Nice country. I like it there.

JOE: What are you studying, I mean, what do you work at, at school?

DALE: I'm studying English. English Literature.

JOE: Yeah? That's a tough racket. I mean, writing. But . . . what? Are you gonna teach? To teach English?

DALE: Oh, I don't know. I'm just . . . studying it because I like it.

JOE: Yeah.

DALE: I may teach.

JOE: Sure, I mean . . . all I mean, it's a tough racket, you know? . . . Hitting the bridge soon?

DALE: Yup.

JOE: How long will you be staying on the boat? About?

DALE: Oh, I don't know. Another month, five weeks.

JOE: Got to go back to school, back East, huh?

DALE: Yeah. I'll leave to go back to school.

JOE: Want a cup? . . . Going back to your studies. Back East. I used to go East. I worked out of Buffalo for a while. I shipped Ford out of Detroit, too. Ford Boats. Ever shipped salt?

DALE: No, you?

JOE: Never did. Always wanted to, though. It's a different life, you know?

DALE: Yeah.

JOE: It must be nice out there. Be pretty easy to ship out. Out of Chicago. I'm an A.B., did you know that? . . . You should get out of Stewards, you know? Get on the deck, get rid of this straightshift crap. If you were on the deck we could go up street at Duluth, Arthur. You'd be out, free, until four in the afternoon and you'd be free at eight and we could fuck around all night, you know? Really hit the bars.

DALE: It's not so bad, really. I have my days free, I get some sun.

JOE: Yeah, but it's not the same thing, it's like having a *job,* for crissakes. I mean, it's okay if you like it.

DALE: It's alright.

JOE: I been working on the Lakes off and on for twenty-three years. It don't seem like such a long time. How old are you, Dale, if you don't mind my asking?

DALE: No, I'm eighteen. Be nineteen in October.

JOE: Yeah? You're a young guy for such a . . . I mean, you're not that *young* but you seem . . . older, you know? You seem like you wouldn't of been that young. Of course, that's not that young. I was working on the boats before I was your age. I'm going to get some more pie. . . . You can see the bridge. You can just make it out. Like a landmark out there. You know, that is one pretty bridge. We been going under that bridge for once or twice a week since I was your age off and on, but that sure is a pretty bridge.

DALE: Yeah, I like it.

JOE: But, I mean, what the fuck? It's a bridge, right? It's something that you use and takes cars from over there over to the island. They don't let no cars drive on that island, did you know that? It's a law. But what I mean, you usually do not think about things that way. From that standpoint. But when you look at it . . . it's just a bridge to get people from the island over to there on the beach . . . you know what I mean.

DALE: Yeah.

JOE: And . . . you go underneath of it and look up and all the same it's pretty. And you forget that it *does* something. But this beauty of it makes what it does all the more . . . nice. Do you know what I'm talking about?

DALE: Yeah, Joe.

JOE: Sometimes I get . . . well, I don't express myself too well, I guess.

DALE: No, I know what you mean.

JOE: You know, you got it made, Dale. You know that? You really got it made.

DALE: What do you mean?

JOE: You got your whole life ahead of you. I mean, you're not a *kid* or anything . . . you're a man. You're a young man. But you got it made.

DALE: What are you talking about, Joe?

JOE: Ah, you know what I'm saying.

DALE: You're not an old man, Joe. What are you talking about?

JOE: Ah, you know what I'm saying to you. I just wanted to tell you, Dale. I just wanted to let you know. So you'll understand. I mean. I've lived longer than you have. And at this stage one can see a lot of things in their proper light. And . . . you're a bright kid.

DALE: Well, sometimes I don't think so.

JOE: Well, what do you know? You know? I mean I've lived a hell of a lot longer than you have and I want to tell you, you're going to be Okay. You're a fine, good-looking kid and you know what's happening. You're okay and you're a good worker. . . . I don't mean that disrespectfully.

DALE: . . . I know.

JOE: And I just want to tell you, sincerely, you have got it made.

DALE: Well.

JOE: No, it's the truth. Christ it's going to be hot today. Going to be a hell of a hot fucking day. Did you make up the First's cabin today?

DALE: Before you came in.

JOE: You don't have to take no shit from him, you know.

DALE: I know that.

JOE: He give you any trouble?

DALE: No, not at all.

JOE: Well, you don't have to take nothing from him. You just do your job. And if he gives you any trouble you talk to the Union Rep when we hit the beach. You know? You just do a good job . . . because that's what he's there for.

DALE: Okay.

JOE: I mean it. If he gives you shit, just let me know.

DALE: Okay, Joe. I'll do that.

JOE: Seriously. We should raise Mackinaw in a couple of minutes. You going up on deck?

DALE: No, I gotta finish up here.

JOE: Yeah, well, I'll see you later. Let me know if you're going up the street, huh?

DALE: I will, Joe.

JOE: We'll hit the bars.

DALE: I will.

JOE: You drink?

(Pause.)

DALE: Yeah.

JOE: Well, I'm going up on the boatdeck. You get off soon, huh?

DALE: In about a half-hour.

JOE: Well, take it easy, Dale. Get some rest. Can you sleep in this heat?

DALE: Easy. I got a scoop out the porthole.

JOE: Oh. Well, it's just that I have trouble sometimes. Well, take it easy, kid.

DALE: Don't work too hard.

JOE: Fuck no. I wouldn't.

Scene 22

Fast Examined

STAN, *on the main deck, buttonholes* COLLINS.

STAN: . . . at least eight. But he doesn't ever draw his gun.
He's giving 'em one of these (whack) and a couple of
these, and some of these, twisting and like a ballet. Till
there's one left. Behind the bar. And all you see: Jonnie's got his back to the bar. We think he thinks this
guy is dead. And you see the guy take this cleaver off
the bar and heft it over his head and just as he starts
to let go, Fast whips around and fires. (Carries this
belly pistol. Black as night. In his *sleeve,* in his fucking
sleeve.) He goes whomp, like that, and the fucking
thing slides down his sleeve and into his hand. And
you see the guy's still got his hand up to throw but all
you see is this little bit of bloody handle. Fast shot the
cleaver out of the guy's fucking hand. BEHIND HIS
BACK. Twenty, thirty feet with a two-inch belly pistol.
Now, how stark is that?

Scene 23

The .38

In the engine room.

FIREMAN: . . . a big black Colt's revolver. A .38 or a .44. Pure blue-black with a black checker grip and an eyelet on the butt for a lanyard—it was an old gun, but in good shape. No scratches. Purest black as a good pair of boots. Must've been re-blued. Or maybe he never used it. You don't know. Used big shells, powerful. You could tell from how big they were. That's a good way to tell. I was in the Army. Overseas. Hawaii. But it wasn't a state. The officers had pistols. They were automatic. .45s. Big heavy things. But his was a re-volver. I've seen it. Shit, he used to take it down here to clean it. He worked down here a while. Don't know how they ever took him. A big guy as quick as he was. I don't see how. Unless they drugged him—or took him from behind.

FRED: I heard they might have drugged him.

FIREMAN: Bastards.

FRED: Or he was drunk.

FIREMAN: Possible. Possible. Very possible. That boy drank. Used to drink on the ship.

FRED: Who doesn't?

FIREMAN: Not him, not him, for sure. No sir, stagger around like an Indian when he had a few. Like a goddamn Winnebago Indian he would.

FRED: That's probably what happened. Did he have his gun with him?

FIREMAN: What'd you hear?

FRED: Didn't hear one way or the other.

FIREMAN: The way I hear it . . . he *took* it. He took the gun to the bar . . . but when they *found* him. HE DIDN'T HAVE IT ON HIM.

FRED: Huh?

FIREMAN: He was a mysterious fellow.

FRED: Huh?

FIREMAN: But he had a lot of gumption.

FRED: I heard that, I didn't know him.

FIREMAN: Yup, a lot of gall.

FRED: Oh yeah.

FIREMAN: I hated that . . . young fellow, what does he know? Blind balls is all. Damn fool like to get killed. Crazy. Crazy, is all. With a big gun like that.

FRED: Maybe he didn't have it on him.

FIREMAN: He had it. I think he had it, by God. I saw him going off and I said to myself, "He looks like trouble.

He just is dripping trouble today. I hope he's got his piece. I just hope, for his own sake that he's got it."

FRED: The cops would know if he had it.

FIREMAN: Or someone could have looked in his stuff.

FRED: They cleaned it out, huh?

FIREMAN: Yeah, been cleaned out. I'd say, for sure. The Mate's responsible.

FRED: Well, whether he took it or not, they got him.

FIREMAN: Fucking cops.

FRED: Yeah . . . why do you say "cops"?

FIREMAN: You kidding? It was the cops got him. Or Uncle Sam.

FRED: The G? What'd the G want with Guiglialli?

FIREMAN: You kidding? With what that kid knew?

FRED: What'd he know?

FIREMAN: Things. He knew things.

FRED: Yeah?

FIREMAN: Surer'n hell, that kid. He'd let on like he didn't know, but he knew. I know when they know. I can see it. And that kid's been around. The cops, they don't like that they find out, they don't sit still. They know. That kid was no cherry, either. He was no dumb kid. I think he was on the run. I think they wanted him.

FRED: The Coast Guard wouldn't let him on the boats if he was wanted. They print you. You know that.

FIREMAN: Still . . .

FRED: How could he get on?

FIREMAN: He had friends. That kid had friends, I tell you. Politics. Strings. You don't know one-half of what he knew. He was no cheap talker, that kid. Talk is cheap.

FRED: You think it was the G, huh?

FIREMAN: I think what I think. That's all I know.

Scene 24

Subterfuge

DALE *is at work in the galley.* JOE *comes in.*

JOE: Hey, Dale. I heard the Steward's in charge of First Aid.

DALE: What's the matter?

JOE: It's just that I heard that. Is it the truth?

DALE: Yup.

JOE: Good. Good. I heard that. What I wanted to know and was wondering, out of curiosity, is: What happens if a guy gets his leg chopped off and they have to give him something? What do they give him?

DALE: Morphine, I guess.

JOE: They keep that stuff on the ship here?

DALE: Not as far as I know. You'd have to ask the Steward.

JOE: Oh, I wouldn't want to have to do that, because I'm just curious. I didn't really want to *know* or anything, you know?

DALE: I understand.

JOE: The Steward's the only one's got keys to First Aid, huh?

DALE: Right.

JOE: Well, alright. Thanks, you know.

(*Pause.*)

But would you do me a favor?

DALE: Sure.

JOE: Would you get me a couple of aspirins and a glass of water?

DALE: Sure, Joe. You got a headache?

JOE: Yeah. I'm not feeling so good the last couple of days.

DALE: What is it?

JOE: I don't know. My back down near my kidneys. It hurts. My head hurts all the time, you know?

DALE: You think it's serious?

JOE: I don't know. It just hurts. It makes you feel old, you know? Sometimes you just get so sick of everything, nothing seems any good, you know? It's all you—don't care . . . Ahhh, it's just me being sick, is all.

DALE: I thought you didn't look right today.

JOE: My hair hurts.

DALE: Mmmmm.

JOE: And my kidney hurts when I walk—I think I'm dying.

DALE: You don't look like you're dying, Joe.

JOE: I sure as hell feel like I am. Sheeeeit.

DALE: Just try to think it won't always be like this, Joe. It's just a temporary illness, in a day or two or a week it'll be all over.

JOE: That's easy for you to say. You don't know what I got.

DALE: What have you got?

JOE: I don't know.

DALE: Well. You can see a doctor the next time we tie up.

JOE: Yeah. It kinda frightens me.

DALE: It does?

JOE: I don't wanna almost find out what I got.

DALE: It's probably nothing serious, Joe. A virus, a little flu or some inflammation, you know?

JOE: Or infection.

DALE: A little infection isn't going to hurt you, Joe. It might only be a touch of stomach flu, something that's going to be over in a day or two. Have you had fever?

JOE: Yeah. At night I been sweating out the sheets terrible. It's inhuman to sleep in them, you know? And I get cold, I don't know. I'm so fucking sick of being sick.

DALE: How long has it been? Four or five days?

JOE: Off and on, yeah, and longer than that.

DALE: You should see a doctor, Joe.

Scene 25

Fingers

JOE *wanders off.* DALE *goes on deck for a cigarette and encounters* FRED *at work.*

FRED: Collucci lost two fingers in the winch.

DALE: Which winch?

FRED: Forward main.

DALE: Who's Collucci?

FRED: Used to ship deck.

DALE: When did he lose them?

FRED: This was a couple, four—five years.

DALE: Yeah.

FRED: He got thirty-six hundred bucks.

DALE: The Company paid him?

FRED: Not counting Workman's Comp and Social Security.

DALE: Do you get Social Security for fingers?

FRED: I don't know. But not counting it he got thirty-six hundred bucks. Eighteen hundred bucks a finger.

DALE: The main winch? Which fingers?

FRED: Right hand. These two.

DALE: That's a bitch. He's crippled.

FRED: Two fingers?

DALE: But the thumb.

FRED: What about it, for thirty-six hundred?

DALE: How could he pick anything up?

FRED: Used the other fucking hand. If they paid him five bucks every time he wanted to pick something up just to use his left hand he'd get . . . thirty-six hundred bucks. . . . For 720 times . . . That's not so much.

DALE: I wouldn't do it.

FRED: He didn't do it on purpose.

DALE: I wouldn't do it at all. Even by accident. No amount of money.

FRED: I think.

DALE: You can't buy a finger, man. It's gone and that's it. Not for all the money in the world.

FRED: Yeah, neither would I.

(SKIPPY *and* COLLINS, *on the bridge, are overheard.*)

SKIPPY: . . . explain it when we don't make schedule on this
watch, you.

COLLINS: I called ahead. They'll have the mail right at the
lock.

Scene 26

Joe's Suicide

DALE, *off watch, is sharing a beer with* JOE *on the boatdeck.*

JOE: You get paid for doing a job. You trade the work for money, am I right? Why is it any fucking less good than being a doctor, for example? That's one thing I never wanted to be, a doctor. I used to want to be lots of things when I was little. You know, like a kid. I wanted to be a ballplayer like everyone. And I wanted to be a cop, what does a kid know, right? And can I tell you something that I wanted to be? I know this is going to sound peculiar, but it was a pure desire on my part. One thing I wanted to be when I was little (I don't mean to be bragging now, or just saying it). If you were there you would have known, it was a pure desire on my part. I wanted to be a dancer. That's one thing I guard. Like you might guard the first time you got laid, or being in love with a girl. Or winning a bike at the movies . . . well, maybe not that. More like getting married, or winning a medal in the war. I wanted to be a dancer. Not tap, I mean a real ballet dancer. I know they're all fags, but I didn't think about it. I didn't *not* think about it. That is, I didn't say, "I want to be a dancer but I do *not* want to be a fag." It

just wasn't important. I saw myself arriving at the theater late doing Swan Lake at the Lyric Opera. With a
coat with one of those old-time collars. (It was winter.)
And on stage with a purple shirt and white tights
catching these girls . . . beautiful light girls. Sweating.
All my muscles are covered in sweat, you know? But
it's clean. And my muscles all feel tight. Every fucking
muscle in my body. Hundreds of them. Tight and
working. And I'm standing up straight on stage with
this kind of expression on my face waiting to catch this
girl. I was about fifteen. It takes a hell of a lot of work
to be a dancer. But a dancer doesn't even fucking care
if he is somebody. He *is* somebody so much so it's not
important. You know what I mean? Like these passengers we get. Guests of the Company. Always being
important. If they're so fucking important, who gives
a fuck? If they're really important why the fuck do they
got to tell you about it?

DALE: I remember in a journalism class in high school the
teacher used to say, never use the word famous in a
story. Like "Mr. X, famous young doctor . . ."

JOE: Right, because if they're fucking famous, why do you
have to say it?

DALE: And he said if they're *not* . . .

JOE: Then what the fuck are you saying it for, right?

DALE: Right.

JOE: It's so fucking obvious you could puke. No class cock-
suckers. You ever try to . . . I don't want to get you
offended by this, you don't have to answer it if you
don't want to.

DALE: No, go ahead.

JOE: I mean, what the fuck? If you're going to talk to somebody, why fuck around the bush, right? Did you ever try to kill yourself?

DALE: No.

JOE: I did one time. I should say that perhaps I shouldn't say I "tried" to kill myself, meaning the gun didn't work. But I wanted to.

DALE: Yeah.

JOE: I had this gun when I lived over on the south side. I won it in a poker game.

DALE: Yeah.

JOE: Aaaaaaah, I fucking bought it off the bumboat in Duluth. Why lie? Forty bucks. A revolver. .32 revolver. Six shots, you know?

DALE: How big a barrel?

JOE: A couple of inches. Like this. I never fired it. One time, coming back, I loaded it and fired one shot off the fantail into the water. I didn't hit anything. I used to clean it. Got this kit in the mail. Patches and oil and gunslick and powder solvent and this brush.

DALE: I've seen them.

JOE: I kept it in my suitcase. One night in Gary, I had this apartment. I was cleaning my gun and, you know how you do, pretending the cops were after me and doing fast draws in the mirror.

DALE: Yeah.

JOE: And I said, "What am I doing? A grown man playing bang bang with a gun in some fucking dive in Gary

Indiana at ten o'clock at night?" And I lay down in front of the TV and loaded the gun. Five chambers. You shouldn't load the sixth in case you jiggle on your horse and blow your foot off.

DALE: Yeah.

JOE: And I put the end in my mouth, and I couldn't swallow and I could feel my pulse start to beat and my balls contract and draw up. You ever feel that?

DALE: No.

JOE: And I took it out of my mouth and laid down on the bed on my back and looked at the ceiling and put the gun under my chin pointing at my brain. But after a while I started feeling really stupid. And I rolled over and put the gun under my pillow, but I still held onto it. And I started. You know, playing with myself, you know what I mean.

DALE: I know.

JOE: A grown man, isn't that something?

Scene 27

Collins and Skippy on the Bridge

COLLINS *has been in control of the boat.* SKIPPY *comes on the bridge.*

SKIPPY: Yo, Mr. Collins.

COLLINS: Yessir.

SKIPPY We pick up the mail?

COLLINS: Yes *sir.*

SKIPPY Good.

COLLINS: We got that report on Guiliani.

SKIPPY That's fine. Get me something to eat.

COLLINS: Yessir. *(Spotting* JOE:*)* Yo, Litko!

JOE: Yo . . . !

Scene 28

In the Galley

Fred: I don't give a fuck; the man lived on the sea, the man
died on the sea.

DALE: He died on land.

FRED: He died 'cause *of* the sea. 'Cause of the sea. 'Cause
of his *trade.* You understand?

DALE: Yeah.

FRED: Good.

(*Pause.*)

DALE: He died 'cause of his desires.

(*Pause.*)

FRED: Yeah.

(*Pause.*)

Well, we all *have* 'em. . . .

(*Pause.*)

DALE: You know him well?

FRED: I knew him *very* well, Dale, *very* well.

(JOE *enters the galley.*)

Yo, Joe . . . !

JOE: Yo, Fred.

FRED: I'm telling my man about Guiliani.

JOE: Yeah. They called the ship. We're picking him up in Duluth.

FRED: We're picking *who* up?

JOE: What?

FRED: *Who* we're picking up?

JOE: Guigliani.

FRED: We're picking up Guigliani?

JOE: Yeah. He caught the train.

FRED: He caught the train to Duluth?

JOE: Yeah.

(*Pause.*)

FRED: How come he missed the boat?

JOE: Yeah. Skippy said he said his aunt died, but he thinks the *real* reason 'cause he overslept.

FRED: . . . sonofabitch . . .

JOE: Well, I'll be glad to have him back.

FRED: *Oh* yeah . . .

DALE: You want a cup of coffee?

JOE: Thank you.

(COLLINS, *on the bridge, is seen talking into the ship-to-shore radio.*)

COLLINS: W.A.Y. Chicago, this is the *T. Harrison* en route.

(*Pause.*)

I read you five-by-five.

EDMOND

To Richard Nelson and Wally Shawn

The world premiere of *Edmond* was produced by the Goodman Theater, Chicago, Illinois, June 4, 1982, with the following cast:

A MISSION PREACHER, A PRISONER	Paul Butler
THE MANAGER, A LEAFLETEER, A CUSTOMER, A POLICEMAN, A GUARD	Rich Cluchey
A B-GIRL, A WHORE	Joyce Hazard
A PEEP SHOW GIRL, GLENNA	Laura Innes
A MAN IN A BAR, A HOTEL CLERK, THE MAN IN BACK, A CHAPLAIN	Bruce Jarchow
EDMOND'S WIFE	Linda Kimbrough
THE FORTUNE-TELLER, A MANAGER, A WOMAN IN THE SUBWAY	Marge Kotlisky
A SHILL, A PIMP	Ernest Perry, Jr.
A CARDSHARP, A GUARD	José Santana
EDMOND	Colin Stinton
A BARTENDER, A BYSTANDER, A PAWNSHOP OWNER, AN INTERROGATOR	Jack Wallace

This production was directed by Gregory Mosher; settings by Bill Bartelt; lighting by Kevin Rigdon; costumes by Marsha Kowal, fight choreography by David Woolley; stage managers, Tom Biscotto and Anne Clarke.

The New York production opened at the Province-town Playhouse on October 27, 1982, with Lionel Mark Smith playing the roles of A SHILL, A PIMP.

Hokey Pokey Wickey Wamm
Salacapinkus Muley Comm
Tamsey Wamsey Wierey Wamm
King of the Cannibal Islands

–Popular Song

Scenes:

Characters:

FORTUNE-TELLER
EDMOND, A MAN IN HIS MID THIRTIES
HIS WIFE
A MAN IN A BAR
A B-GIRL
A BARTENDER
THE MANAGER
A PEEP-SHOW GIRL
THREE GAMBLERS
A CARD SHARP
A BYSTANDER
TWO SHILLS
A LEAFLETEER
A MANAGER (F)
A WHORE
A HOTEL CLERK
A PAWNSHOP OWNER
A CUSTOMER
THE MAN IN BACK
A WOMAN ON THE SUBWAY
A PIMP
GLENNA, A WAITRESS
A TRAMP
A MISSION PREACHER
A POLICEMAN
AN INTERROGATOR
A PRISONER

A CHAPLAIN
A GUARD

Setting:

New York City

Scene 1

The Fortune-Teller

EDMOND *and the* FORTUNE-TELLER *seated across the table from each other.*

FORTUNE-TELLER: If things are predetermined surely they must manifest themselves.
When we look back—as we look back—we see that we could never have done otherwise than as we did. (*Pause.*)
Surely, then, there must have been signs.
If only we could have read them. We say, "I see now that I could not have done otherwise . . . my *diet* caused me. Or my stars . . . which caused me to eat what I ate . . . or my *genes,* or some other thing beyond my control forced me to act as I did . . ."
And those things which *forced* us, of course, must make their signs: our *diet,* or our *genes,* or our *stars.*

(*Pause.*)

And there *are* signs. (*Pause.*)
What we see reflects (more than what is) what is to be.

(*Pause.*)

Are you cold?

EDMOND: No. *(Pause.)*

FORTUNE-TELLER: Would you like me to close the window?

EDMOND: No, thank you.

FORTUNE-TELLER: Give me your palm.

*(*EDMOND *does so.)*

You are not where you belong. It is perhaps true none of us are, but in your case this is more true than in most.
We all like to believe we are special. In your case this is true.
Listen to me. *(She continues talking as the lights dim.)*
The world seems to be crumbling around us. You look and you wonder if what you perceive is accurate. And you are unsure what your place is. To what extent you are cause and to what an effect. . . .

Scene 2

At Home

EDMOND *and his* WIFE *are sitting in the living room. A pause.*

WIFE: The girl broke the lamp. *(Pause.)*

EDMOND: Which lamp?

WIFE: The antique lamp.

EDMOND: In my room?

WIFE: Yes. *(Pause.)*

EDMOND: Huh.

WIFE: That lamp cost over two hundred and twenty dollars.

EDMOND *(pause):* Maybe we can get it fixed.

WIFE: We're never going to get it fixed,
I think that that's the *point.* . . .
I think that's why she did it.

EDMOND: Yes. Alright—I'm going. *(Pause. He gets up and starts out of the room.)*

WIFE: Will you bring me back some cigarettes. . . .

EDMOND: I'm not coming back.

WIFE: What?

EDMOND: I'm not coming back. *(Pause.)*

WIFE: What do you mean?

EDMOND: I'm going, and I'm not going to come back. *(Pause.)*

WIFE: You're not *ever* coming back?

EDMOND: No.

WIFE: Why not? *(Pause.)*

EDMOND: I don't want to live this kind of life.

WIFE: What does that mean?

EDMOND: That I can't live this life.

WIFE: "You can't live this life" so you're leaving me.

EDMOND: Yes.

WIFE: Ah. Ah. Ah.
And what about ME?
Don't you *love* me anymore?

EDMOND: No.

WIFE: You don't.

EDMOND: No.

WIFE: And why is that?

EDMOND: I don't know.

WIFE: And when did you find this out?

EDMOND: A long time ago.

WIFE: You did.

EDMOND: Yes.

WIFE: How long ago?

EDMOND: Years ago.

WIFE: You've known for years that you don't love me.

EDMOND: Yes. *(Pause.)*

WIFE: Oh. *(Pause.)* Then why did you decide you're leaving *now?*

EDMOND: I've had enough.

WIFE: Yes. But why *now?*

EDMOND *(pause):* Because you don't interest me spiritually
   or sexually. *(Pause.)*

WIFE: Hadn't you known this for some time?

EDMOND: What do you think?

WIFE: I think you did.

EDMOND: Yes, I did.

WIFE: And why didn't you leave *then?*
   Why didn't you leave *then,* you stupid *shit!!!*
   All of these years you say that you've been living
   here? . . .

   (Pause.)

   Eh? You idiot. . . .
   I've had enough.
   You idiot . . . to see you passing *judgment* on me all this
   time . . .

EDMOND: . . . I never judged you. . . .

WIFE: . . . and then you tell me. "You're leaving."

EDMOND: Yes.

WIFE: *Go,* then. . . .

EDMOND: I'll call you.

WIFE: Please. And we'll talk. What shall we do with the house? Cut it in half?
Go. Get out of here. Go.

EDMOND: You think that I'm fooling.

WIFE: I do *not.* Good-bye. Thank you. Good-bye.
(Pause.) Good-bye. *(Pause.)*
Get *out.* Get *out* of here.
And don't you *ever* come back.
Do you hear me?

(WIFE exits. Closing the door on him.)

Scene 3

A Bar

EDMOND *is at the bar. A* MAN *is next to him. They sit for a while.*

MAN: . . . I'll tell you who's got it *easy.* . . .

EDMOND: Who?

MAN: The niggers. *(Pause.)* Sometimes I wish I was a nigger.

EDMOND: Sometimes I do, too.

MAN: I'd rob a store. I don't blame them.
I swear to God. Because I want to tell you: we're *bred* to do the things that we do.

EDMOND: Mm.

MAN: Northern races *one* thing, and the southern races something else. And what *they* want to do is sit beneath the tree and watch the elephant. *(Pause.)* And I don't blame them one small bit. Because there's too much *pressure* on us.

EDMOND: Yes.

MAN: And that's no joke, and that's not *poetry,* it's just too much.

EDMOND: It is. It absolutely is.

MAN: A man's got to get *out.* . . .

EDMOND: What do you mean?

MAN: A man's got to get *away* from himself. . . .

EDMOND: . . . that's true . . .

MAN: . . . because the pressure is too much.

EDMOND: What do you do?

MAN: What do you mean?

EDMOND: What do you do to get out?

MAN: What do I do?

EDMOND: Yes.

MAN: What are the things to do? What are the things *anyone* does? . . . *(Pause.)*
Pussy . . . I don't know. . . . *Pussy* . . . *Power* . . . *Money* . . . uh . . . *adventure* . . . *(Pause.)*
I think that's it . . . uh, self-*destruction* . . .
I think that that's it . . . don't you? . . .

EDMOND: Yes.

MAN: . . . uh, *religion* . . . I suppose that's it, uh, *release,* uh, ratification. *(Pause.)*
You have to get *out,* you have to get something opens your *nose,* life is too short.

EDMOND: My wife and I are incompatible.

MAN: I'm sorry to hear that. *(Pause.)*
In what way?

EDMOND: I don't find her attractive.

MAN: Mm.

EDMOND: It's a boring thing to talk about. But that's what's on my mind.

MAN: I understand.

EDMOND: You do?

MAN: Yes. *(Pause.)*

EDMOND: Thank you.

MAN: Believe me, that's alright. I know that we all *need* it, and we don't know where to *get* it, and I know what it *means,* and I understand.

EDMOND: . . . I feel . . .

MAN: I know. Like your balls were cut off.

EDMOND: Yes. A long, long time ago.

MAN: Mm-hm.

EDMOND: And I don't feel like a man.

MAN: Do you know what you need?

EDMOND: No.

MAN: You need to get laid.

EDMOND: I do. I know I do.

MAN: That's why the niggers have it easy.

EDMOND: Why?

MAN: I'll tell you why: there are responsibilities they never have accepted. *(Pause.)*
Try the Allegro.

EDMOND: What is that?

MAN: A bar on Forty-seventh Street.

EDMOND: Thank you.

(The MAN *gets up, pays for drinks.)*

MAN: I want this to be on me. I want you to *remember* there
was someone who listened. *(Pause.)*
You'd do the same for me.

(The MAN *exits.)*

Scene 4

The Allegro

EDMOND *sits by himself for a minute. A* B-GIRL *comes by.*

B-GIRL: You want to buy me a drink?

EDMOND: Yes. *(Pause.)*
I'm putting myself at your *mercy* . . . this is my first time in a place like this. I don't want to be taken advantage of.

(Pause.)

You understand?

B-GIRL: Buy me a drink and we'll go in the back.

EDMOND: And do what?

B-GIRL: Whatever you want.

*(*EDMOND *leans over and whispers to* B-GIRL.*)*

B-GIRL: Ten dollars.

EDMOND: Alright.

B-GIRL: Buy me a drink.

EDMOND: You get a commission on the drinks?

B-GIRL: Yes.

(She gestures to BARTENDER, *who brings drinks.)*

EDMOND: How much commission do you get?

B-GIRL: Fifty percent.

BARTENDER *(bringing drinks):* That's twenty bucks.

EDMOND *(getting up):* It's too much.

BARTENDER: What?

EDMOND: Too much. Thank you.

B-GIRL: Ten!

EDMOND: No, thank you.

B-GIRL: Ten!

EDMOND: I'll give you five. I'll give you the five you'd get
for the drink if I gave them ten.
But I'm not going to give them ten.

B-GIRL: But you have to buy me a drink.

EDMOND: I'm sorry. No.

B-GIRL: Alright. *(Pause.)* Give me ten.

EDMOND: On top of the ten?

B-GIRL: Yeah. You give me twenty.

EDMOND: I should give you twenty.

B-GIRL: Yes.

EDMOND: To *you.*

B-Girl: Yes.

Edmond: And then you give him the five?

B-Girl: Yes. I got to give him the five.

Edmond: No.

B-Girl: For the *drink.*

Edmond: No. You don't have to pay him for the drink.
It's *tea* . . .

B-Girl: It's not tea.

Edmond: It's not tea!? . . .

(*He drinks.*)

If it's not *tea* what *is* it, then? . . .
I came here to be *straight* with you, why do we have to
go *through* this? . . .

Manager: Get in or get out. (*Pause.*)
Don't mill around.
Get in or get out . . . (*Pause.*)
Alright.

(**Manager** *escorts* **Edmond** *out of the bar.*)

Scene 5

A Peep Show

Booths with closed doors all around. A GIRL *in a spangled leotard sees* EDMOND *and motions him to a booth whose door she is opening.*

GIRL: Seven. Go in Seven. *(He starts to Booth Seven.)*
   No. Six! I mean Six. Go in Six.

   (He goes into Booth Six. She disappears behind the row of booths, and appears behind a plexiglass partition in Booth Six.)

   Take your dick out. *(Pause.)*
   Take your dick out. *(Pause.)*
   Come on. Take your dick out.

EDMOND: I'm not a cop.

GIRL: I know you're not a cop. Take your dick out.
   I'm gonna give you a good time.

EDMOND: How can we get this barrier to come down?

GIRL: It doesn't come down.

EDMOND: Then how are you going to give me a good time?

GIRL: Come here.

(He leans close. She whispers.)

Give me ten bucks. *(Pause.)*
Give me ten bucks. *(Pause.)*
Put it through the thing.

(She indicates a small ventilator hole in the plexiglass. Pause.)

Put it through the thing.

EDMOND *(checking his wallet):* I haven't got ten bucks.

GIRL: Okay . . . just . . . yes.
Okay. Give me the twenty.

EDMOND: Are you going to give me change?

GIRL: Yes. Just give me the twenty. Give it to me.
Good. Now take your dick out.

EDMOND: Can I have my ten?

GIRL: Look. Let me hold the ten.

EDMOND: Give me my ten back. *(Pause.)*
Come on. Give me my ten back.

GIRL: Let me hold the ten. . . .

EDMOND: Give me my ten back and I'll give you a tip when
you're done.

(Pause. She does so.)

Thank you.

GIRL: Okay. Take your dick out.

EDMOND *(of the plexiglass):* How does this thing come down?

GIRL: It doesn't come down.

EDMOND: It doesn't come down?

GIRL: No.

EDMOND: Then what the fuck am I giving you ten bucks for?

GIRL: Look: You can touch me. Stick your finger in this you can touch me.

EDMOND: I don't want to touch *you.* . . .
I want *you* to touch *me.* . . .

GIRL: I can't. *(Pause.)* I would, but I can't. We'd have the cops in here. We would.
Honestly. *(Pause.)*
Look: Put your finger in here . . . come on.
(Pause.) Come on.

(He zips his pants up and leaves the booth.)

You're only cheating your*self.* . . .

Scene 6

On the Street, Three-Card Monte

A CARDSHARP, *a* BYSTANDER *and* TWO SHILLS.

SHARPER: You pick the red you win, and twenty get you
forty. Put your money up.
The *black* gets *back*, the *red* you go ahead. . . .
Who saw the red? . . . Who saw the red?
Who saw her? . . .

BYSTANDER *(to* EDMOND*):* The fellow over there is a
shill . . .

EDMOND: Who is? . . .

BYSTANDER *(points):* You want to know how to beat the
game?

EDMOND: How?

BYSTANDER: You figure out which card has *got* to win. . . .

EDMOND: . . . Uh-huh . . .

BYSTANDER: . . . and bet the *other* one.

SHARPER: Who saw the red? . . .

BYSTANDER: They're all shills, they're all part of an act.

SHARPER: Who saw her? Five will get you ten. . . .

SHILL *(playing lookout):* Cops . . . cops . . . cops . . . *don't* run
. . . *don't* run. . . .

(Everyone scatters. EDMOND *moves down the street.)*

Scene 7

Passing Out Leaflets

EDMOND *moves down the street. A* MAN *is passing out leaflets.*

LEAFLETEER: Check it out . . . check it out. . . .
   This is what you looking for. . . . Take it . . .
   I'm *giving* you something. . . . *Take* it. . . .

   (EDMOND *takes the leaflet.*)

   Now: Is that what you looking for or not? . . .

EDMOND *(reading the leaflet):* Is this true? . . .

LEAFLETEER: Would I give it to you if it wasn't? . . .

   (EDMOND *walks off reading the leaflet. The* LEAFLETEER
   continues with his spiel.)

   Check it out. . . .

Scene 8

The Whorehouse

EDMOND *shows up with the leaflet. He talks to the* MANAGER, *a woman.*

MANAGER: Hello.

EDMOND: Hello.

MANAGER: Have you been here before?

EDMOND: No.

MANAGER: How'd you hear about us? (EDMOND *shows her the leaflet.*) You from out of town?

EDMOND: Yes. What's the deal here?

MANAGER: This is a *health* club.

EDMOND: . . . I know.

MANAGER: And our rates are by the hour. (*Pause.*)

EDMOND: Yes?

MANAGER: Sixty-eight dollars for the first hour, sauna, free bar, showers . . . (*Pause.*)
The hour doesn't start until you and the masseuse are in the room.

EDMOND: Alright.

MANAGER: Whatever happens in the room, of course, is between you.

EDMOND: I understand.

MANAGER: You understand?

EDMOND: Yes.

MANAGER: . . . Or, for two hours it's one hundred fifty dollars. If you want two hostesses that is two hundred dollars for one hour. *(Pause.)* Whatever arrangement that you choose to make with *them* is between *you.*

EDMOND: Good. *(Pause.)*

MANAGER: What would you like?

EDMOND: One hour.

MANAGER: You pay that now. How would you like to pay?

EDMOND: How can I pay?

MANAGER: With cash or credit card. The billing for the card will read "Atlantic Ski and Tennis."

EDMOND: I'll pay you with cash.

Scene 9

Upstairs at the Whorehouse

EDMOND *and the* WHORE *are in a cubicle.*

WHORE: How are you?

EDMOND: Fine. I've never done this before.

WHORE: No? *(She starts rubbing his neck.)*

EDMOND: No. That feels very good. *(Pause.)*

WHORE: You've got a good body.

EDMOND: Thank you.

WHORE: Do you work out? *(Pause.)*

EDMOND: I jog.

WHORE: Mmm. *(Pause.)*

EDMOND: And I used to play football in high school.

WHORE: You've kept yourself in good shape.

EDMOND: Thank you.

WHORE *(pause):* What shall we do?

EDMOND: I'd like to have intercourse with you.

WHORE: That sounds very nice. I'd like that, too.

EDMOND: You would?

WHORE: Yes.

EDMOND: How much would that be?

WHORE: For a straight fuck, that would be a hundred fifty.

EDMOND: That's too much.

WHORE: You know that I'm giving you a break. . . .

EDMOND: . . . no . . .

WHORE: . . . Because this is your first time here. . . .

EDMOND: No. It's too much, on top of the sixty-eight at the
    door. . . .

WHORE: . . . I know, I know, but you know, I don't get to
    keep it all. I *split* it with them. Yes. They don't pay me,
    I pay *them.*

EDMOND: It's too much. *(Pause. The* WHORE *sighs.)*

WHORE: How much do you have?

EDMOND: All I had was one hundred for the whole thing.

WHORE: You mean a hundred for it all.

EDMOND: That only left me thirty.

WHORE: Noooo, honey, you couldn't get a *thing* for that.

EDMOND: Well, how much do you want?

WHORE *(sighs):* Alright, for a straight fuck, one hundred
    twenty.

EDMOND: I couldn't pay that.

WHORE: I'm sorry, then. It would have been nice.

EDMOND: I'll give you eighty.

WHORE: No.

EDMOND: One hundred.

WHORE: Alright, but only, you know, 'cause this is your first time.

EDMOND: I know.

WHORE: . . . 'cause we *split* with them, you understand. . . .

EDMOND: I understand.

WHORE: Alright. One hundred.

EDMOND: Thank you. I appreciate this. *(Pause.)* Would it offend you if I wore a rubber? . . .

WHORE: Not at all. *(Pause.)*

EDMOND: Do you have one? . . .

WHORE: Yes. *(Pause.)* You want to pay me now? . . .

EDMOND: Yes. Certainly. *(He takes out his wallet, hands her a credit card.)*

WHORE: I need cash, honey.

EDMOND: They said at the door I could pay with my . . .

WHORE: . . . That was at the door . . . you have to pay *me* with *cash.* . . .

EDMOND: I don't think I *have* it. . . . *(He checks through his wallet.)* I don't *have* it. . . .

WHORE: How much do you have? . . .

EDMOND: I, uh, only have *sixty.*

WHORE: Jeez, I'm *sorry,* honey, but I can't *do* it. . . .

EDMOND: Well, wait, wait, wait, wait, maybe we could
. . . wait. . . .

WHORE: Why don't you *get* it, and come *back* here. . . .

EDMOND: Well, where could I *get* it? . . .

WHORE: Go to a restaurant and cash a check, I'll be here
till *four.* . . .

EDMOND: I'll. I'll . . . um, um . . . *yes. Thank* you. . . .

WHORE: Not at all.

(EDMOND *leaves the whorehouse.)*

Scene 10

Three-Card Monte

EDMOND *out on the street, passes by the three-card-monte men, who have assembled again.*

SHARPER: You can't win if you don't play. . . . (*To* EDMOND:)
You, sir . . .

EDMOND: Me? . . .

SHARPER: You going to try me again? . . .

EDMOND: Again? . . .

SHARPER: *I* remember you beat me out of that *fifty* that time with your girlfriend. . . .

EDMOND: . . . When was this?

SHARPER: On four*teen*ff street. . . .
You going to try me one more time? . . .

EDMOND: Uh . . .

SHARPER: . . . Play you for that fifty. . . . Fifty get you one hundred, we see you as fast as you was. . . .
Pay on the red, pass on the black. . . .
Where is the queen? . . . You pick the queen you win. . . .

Where is the queen? . . . Who saw the queen? . . . You put up fifty, win a hundred. . . . Now: Who saw the queen? . . .

SHILL: I got her!

SHARPER: How much? Put your money up. How much?

SHILL: I bet you fifty dollars.

SHARPER: Put it up.

(The SHILL *does so. The* SHILL *turns a card.)*

SHILL: There!

SHARPER: My man, I'm jus' too quick for you today. *Who* saw the queen? We got two cards left. Pay on the *red* queen, who saw her?

EDMOND: I saw her.

SHARPER: Ah, *shit,* man, you too fass for me.

EDMOND: . . . For fifty dollars . . .

SHARPER: Alright—alright. Put it up. *(Pause.)*

EDMOND: Will you pay me if I win?

SHARPER: Yes, I will. If you win. But you got to *win* first. . . .

EDMOND: All that I've got to do is turn the queen.

SHARPER: Thass all you got to do.

EDMOND: I'll bet you fifty.

SHARPER: You sure?

EDMOND: Yes. I'm sure.

SHARPER: Put it up. (EDMOND *does so.*) Now: Which one you like?

EDMOND *(turning card):* There!

SHARPER *(taking money):* I'm *sorry,* my man. This time you lose—
now we even. Take another shot. You pick the queen you win . . . bet you another fifty. . . .

EDMOND: Let me see those cards.

SHARPER: These cards are fine, it's you thass slow.

EDMOND: I want to see the cards.

SHARPER: These cards are good my man, you *lost.*

EDMOND: You let me see those cards.

SHARPER: You ain't goin' *see* no motherfuckin' cards, man, we playin' a *game* here. . . .

SHILL: . . . You lost, *get* lost.

EDMOND: Give me those cards, fella.

SHARPER: You want to see the cards? You want to see the cards? . . . *Here* is the motherfuckin' cards. . . .

(He hits EDMOND in the face. He and the SHILL beat ED-MOND for several seconds. EDMOND falls to the ground.)

Scene 11

A Hotel

EDMOND, *torn and battered, comes up to the* DESK CLERK.

EDMOND: I want a room.

CLERK: Twenty-two dollars. *(Pause.)*

EDMOND: I lost my wallet.

CLERK: Go to the police.

EDMOND: You can call up American Express.

CLERK: Go to the police. *(Pause.)*
    I don't want to hear it.

EDMOND: You can call the credit-card people. I have insur-
    ance.

CLERK: Call them yourself. Right across the hall.

EDMOND: I have no money.

CLERK: I'm sure it's a free call.

EDMOND: Do those phones require a dime?

CLERK *(Pause):* I'm sure I don't know.

EDMOND: You know if they need a *dime* or not.
    To get a *dial* tone . . . You know if they need a *dime,* for chrissake. Do you want to live in this kind of world? Do you want to live in a *world* like that? I've been *hurt?* Are you *blind?* Would you appreciate it if I acted this way to *you? (Pause.)*
    I *asked* you one simple thing.
    Do they need a *dime?*

CLERK: No. They don't need a dime. Now, you make your call, and you go somewhere else.

Scene 12

The Pawnshop

The OWNER *waiting on a customer who is perusing objects in the display counter.*

CUSTOMER: Whaddaya get for that? What is that? Fourteen or eighteen karat?

OWNER: Fourteen.

CUSTOMER: Yeah? Lemme see that. How much is that?

OWNER: Six hundred eighty-five.

CUSTOMER: Why is that? How old is that? Is that *old?*

OWNER: You know how much *gold* that you got in there? Feel. That. Just feel that.

CUSTOMER: Where is it marked?

OWNER: Right there. You want that loupe?

CUSTOMER: No. I can see it.

(EDMOND *comes into the store and stands by the two.*)

OWNER (*to* Edmond): What?

EDMOND: I want to pawn something.

OWNER: Talk to the man in back.

CUSTOMER: What else you got like this?

OWNER: I don't know *what* I got. You're *looking* at it.

CUSTOMER *(pointing to item in display case):* Lemme see that.

EDMOND *(goes to* MAN *in back behind grate):* I want to pawn
   something.

MAN: What?

EDMOND: My ring. *(Holds up hand.)*

MAN: Take it off.

EDMOND: It's difficult to take it off.

MAN: Spit on it. (EDMOND *does so.)*

CUSTOMER: How much is that?

OWNER: Two hundred twenty.

EDMOND *(happily):* I got it off. *(He hands the ring to the* MAN.*)*

MAN: What do you want to do with this?
   You want to pawn it.

EDMOND: Yes. How does that work?

MAN: Is that what you want to do?

EDMOND: Yes. Are there other things to do?

MAN: . . . What you can *do,* no, I mean, if you wanted it
   appraised . . .

EDMOND: . . . Uh-huh . . .

MAN: . . . or want to *sell* it . . .

EDMOND: . . . Uh-huh . . .

MAN: . . . or you wanted it to *pawn*. . . .

EDMOND: I understand.

MAN: Alright?

EDMOND: How much is getting it appraised?

MAN: Five dollars.

CUSTOMER: Lemme see something in black.

EDMOND: What would you give me if I pawned it?

MAN: What do you want for it?

EDMOND: What is it worth?

MAN: You pawn it all you're gonna get's approximately . . . You know how this works?

CUSTOMER: Yes. Let me see that. . . .

EDMOND: No.

MAN: What you get, a quarter of the value.

EDMOND: Mm.

MAN: Approximately. For a year. You're paying twelve percent. You can redeem your pledge with the year you pay your twelve percent. To that time. Plus the amount of the loan.

EDMOND: What is my pledge?

MAN: Well, that depends on what it *is*.

EDMOND: What do you mean?

MAN: What it *is*. Do you understand?

EDMOND: No.

MAN: Whatever the amount *is*, that is your pledge.

EDMOND: The amount of the loan.

MAN: That's right.

EDMOND: I understand.

MAN: Alright. What are you looking for, the ring?

CUSTOMER: Nope. Not today. I'll catch you next time. Lemme see that knife.

EDMOND: What is it worth?

MAN: The most I can give you, hundred and twenty bucks.

CUSTOMER: This is nice.

EDMOND: I'll take it.

MAN: Good. I'll be right back. Give me the ring.

(EDMOND *does so.* EDMOND *wanders over to watch the other transaction.*)

CUSTOMER *(holding up knife):* What are you asking for this?

OWNER: Twenty-three bucks. Say, twenty bucks.

CUSTOMER *(to himself):* Twenty bucks . . .

EDMOND: Why is it so expensive?

OWNER: Why is it so expensive?

CUSTOMER: No. I'm going to pass. *(He hands knife back, exiting.)* I'll catch you later.

OWNER: Right.

EDMOND: Why is the knife so expensive?

OWNER: This is a *survival* knife. G. I. Issue. World War Two. And that is why.

EDMOND: Survival knife.

OWNER: That is correct.

EDMOND: Is it a good knife?

OWNER: It is the best knife that money can buy.

(He starts to put knife away. As an afterthought:)

You want it?

EDMOND: Let me think about it for a moment.

Scene 13

The Subway

EDMOND *is in the subway. Waiting with him is a* WOMAN *in a hat.*

EDMOND *(Pause):* My mother had a hat like that. *(Pause.)* My mother had a hat like that. *(Pause.)* I . . . I'm not making conversation. She wore it for years. She had it when I was a child.

(The WOMAN *starts to walk away.* EDMOND *grabs her.)*

I wasn't just making it *up.* It *happened.* . . .

WOMAN *(detaching herself from his grip):* Excuse me. . . .

EDMOND: . . . who the fuck do you think you *are?* . . . I'm *talking* to you . . . What am I? A *stone?* . . . Did I say, "I want to lick your pussy"? . . . I said, "My mother had that same hat. . . ." You *cunt* . . . What am I? A *dog?* I'd like to slash your fucking *face* . . . I'd like to slash your motherfucking *face* apart. . . .

WOMAN: . . . WILL SOMEBODY *HELP ME.* . . .

EDMOND: *You* don't know who I am. . . . *(She breaks free.)*
Is everybody in this town *insane?* . . . Fuck you . . . fuck
you . . . fuck you . . . fuck the *lot* of you . . . fuck you
all . . . I don't *need* you . . . I worked all of my life!

Scene 14

On the Street, outside the Peep Show

Pimp: What are you looking for?

Edmond: What?

Pimp: What are you looking for?

Edmond: I'm not looking for a goddamn thing.

Pimp: You looking for that *joint,* it's *closed.*

Edmond: What joint?

Pimp: That *joint* that you was looking for.

Edmond: Thank you, no. I'm not looking for that joint.

Pimp: You looking for *something,* and I think that I know what you looking for.

Edmond: You do?

Pimp: You come with me, I get you what you want.

Edmond: What do I want?

Pimp: *I* know. We get you some *action,* my friend.
We get you something sweet to shoot on. *(Pause.)*
I know. Thass what I'm doing here.

EDMOND: What are you saying?

PIMP: I'm saying that we going to find you something nice.

EDMOND: You're saying that you're going to find me a
    woman.

PIMP: Thass what I'm *doing* out here, friend.

EDMOND: How much?

PIMP: Well, how much do you want?

EDMOND: I want somebody clean.

PIMP: Thass right.

EDMOND: I want a blow-job.

PIMP: Alright.

EDMOND: How much?

PIMP: Thirty bucks.

EDMOND: That's too much.

PIMP: How much do you want to *spen'*? . . .

EDMOND: Say fifteen dollars.

PIMP: Twenny-five.

EDMOND: No. Twenty.

PIMP: Yes.

EDMOND: Is that alright?

PIMP: Give me the twenty.

EDMOND: I'll give it to you when we see the girl.

PIMP: Hey, I'm not going to *leave* you, man, you *coming* with me. We *goin'* to see the girl.

EDMOND: Good. I'll give it to you then.

PIMP: You give it to me *now*, you unnerstan'? Huh? *Pause.)* Thass the trans*action. (Pause.)* You see? Unless you were a *cop. (Pause.)* You give me the *money*, and then thass en*trap*ment. *(Pause.)* You understand?

EDMOND: Yes. I'm not a cop.

PIMP: Alright.
Do you *see* what I'm saying?

EDMOND: I'm sorry.

PIMP: Thass alright. (EDMOND *takes out wallet. Exchange of money.)* You come with me. Now we'll just walk here like we're talking.

EDMOND: Is she going to be clean?

PIMP: Yes, she is. I understand you, man.

(Pause. They walk.)

I understand what you want. *(Pause.)* Believe me.

(Pause.)

EDMOND: Is there any money in this?

PIMP: Well, you know, man, there's *some* . . . you get done piecing off the *police*, this man *here* . . . the *medical*, the *bills, you* know.

EDMOND: How much does the girl get?

PIMP: Sixty percent.

EDMOND: Mm.

PIMP: *Oh* yeah. *(He indicates a spot.)* Up here.

(They walk to the spot. The PIMP *takes out a knife and holds it to* EDMOND'*s neck.)*

Now give me all you' money mothafucka! *Now!*

EDMOND: Alright.

PIMP: *All* of it. Don't turn aroun' . . . don't turn aroun' . . . just put it in my hand.

EDMOND: Alright.

PIMP: . . . And don't you make a motherfuckin' sound. . . .

EDMOND: I'm going to do everything that you say. . . .

PIMP: Now you just han' me all you got.

*(*EDMOND *turns, strikes the* PIMP *in the face.)*

EDMOND: YOU MOTHERFUCKING NIGGER!

PIMP: Hold on. . . .

EDMOND: You motherfucking *shit* . . . you *jungle* bunny . . . *(He strikes the* PIMP *again. He drops his knife.)*

PIMP: I . . .

EDMOND: You *coon,* you *cunt,* you *cock*sucker . . .

PIMP: I . . .

EDMOND: "Take me upstairs"? . . .

Pɪᴍᴘ: Oh, my God . . . (*The* Pɪᴍᴘ *has fallen to the sidewalk and* Eᴅᴍᴏɴᴅ *is kicking him.*)

Eᴅᴍᴏɴᴅ: You *fuck.* You *nigger.* You dumb *cunt . . .*
  You *shit . . .* You shit . . . (*Pause.*)
  You fucking *nigger.* (*Pause.*) Don't fuck with *me,* you
  coon. . . .

  (*Pause.* Eᴅᴍᴏɴᴅ *spits on him.*)

  I hope you're *dead.*

  (*Pause.*)

  Don't fuck with *me,* you *coon. . . .*

  (*Pause.* Eᴅᴍᴏɴᴅ *spits on him.*)

Scene 15

The Coffeehouse

EDMOND *seated in the coffeehouse, addresses the waitress,* GLENNA.

EDMOND: I want a cup of coffee. No. A beer.
　　Beer chaser. Irish whiskey.

GLENNA: Irish whiskey.

EDMOND: Yes. A double. Huh.

GLENNA: You're in a peppy mood today.

EDMOND: You're goddamn right I am, and you want me to
　　tell you *why?* Because I am *alive.* You know how much
　　of our life we're alive, you and me? *Nothing.* Two min-
　　utes out of the year. You know, you know, we're *shel-
　　tered.* . . .

GLENNA: Who is?

EDMOND: You and I. White people. All of us. All of us.
　　We're doomed. The white race is doomed. And do
　　you know *why?* . . . Sit down. . . .

GLENNA: I can't. I'm working.

EDMOND: And do you know *why*—you can do anything you
　　want to do, you don't sit down because you're *"work-

ing," the reason you don't sit down is you don't *want* to sit down, because it's more comfortable to *accept* a law than question it and live your life. All of us. *All* of us.

We've bred the life out of ourselves. And we live in a fog.

We live in a dream. Our life is a *school*house, and we're dead.

(Pause.)

How old are you?

GLENNA: Twenty-eight.

EDMOND: I've lived in a fog for thirty-four years. Most of the life I have to live. It's gone. It's gone. I wasted it. Because I didn't know. And you know what the answer is? To *live. (Pause.) I want to go home with you tonight.*

GLENNA: Why?

EDMOND: Why do you think? I want to fuck you. *(Pause.)* It's as simple as that. What's your name?

GLENNA: Glenna. *(Pause.)* What's yours?

EDMOND: Edmond.

Scene 16

Glenna's Apartment

EDMOND *and* GLENNA *are lounging around semiclothed.* ED-MOND *shows* GLENNA *the survival knife.*

EDMOND: You see this?

GLENNA: Yes.

EDMOND: That fucking nigger comes up to me, what am I fitted to do. He comes up, "Give me all your money." Thirty-four years fits me to sweat and say he's under-paid, and he can't get a *job*, he's *bigger* than me . . . he's a *killer*, he don't care about his *life*, you understand, so he'd do *anything*. . . .
Eh? That's what I'm fitted to do. In a mess of intellec-tuality to wet my *pants* while this *coon* cuts my *dick* off . . . eh? Because I'm taught to *hate*.
I want to tell you something. Something *spoke* to me, I got a *shock* (I don't know, I got mad . . .), I got a *shock*, and I spoke *back* to him. "Up your *ass*, you *coon* . . . you want to fight, *I'll* fight you, I'll cut out your fuckin' *heart*, eh, *I* don't give a fuck. . . ."

GLENNA: Yes.

EDMOND: Eh? I'm saying, *"I* don't give a fuck, *I* got some warlike blood in *my* veins, too, you fucking *spade,* you coon. . . ." The *blood* ran down his neck. . . .

GLENNA *(looking at knife):* With *that?*

EDMOND: You bet your ass. . . .

GLENNA: Did you kill him?

EDMOND: Did I kill him?

GLENNA: Yes.

EDMOND: I don't care. *(Pause.)*

GLENNA: That's wonderful.

EDMOND: And in that *moment* . . .
    when I *spoke,* you understand, 'cause that was more important than the *knife,* when I spoke *back* to him, I DIDN'T FUCKING WANT TO *UNDERSTAND* . . . let *him* understand *me* . . .
    I wanted to KILL him. *(Pause.)* In that *moment* thirty years of prejudice came out of me. *(Pause.)* Thirty *years.* Of all those um um um of all those *cleaning* ladies . . .

GLENNA: . . . Uh-huh . . .

EDMOND: . . . uh? . . . who *might* have broke the lamp. SO WHAT? You understand? For the first *time,* I swear to God, for the first *time* I saw: THEY'RE PEOPLE, TOO.

GLENNA *(pause):* Do you know who I hate?

EDMOND: Who is that?

GLENNA: Faggots.

EDMOND: Yes. I hate them, too. And you know *why?*

GLENNA: Why?

EDMOND: They suck cock. *(Pause.)* And that's the truest thing you'll ever hear.

GLENNA: I hate them 'cause they don't like women.

EDMOND: They *hate* women.

GLENNA: I know that they do.

EDMOND: It makes you feel good to *say* it? Doesn't it?

GLENNA: Yes.

EDMOND: Then *say* it. *Say* it. If it makes you whole. *Always* say it. *Always* for your*self* . . .

GLENNA: It's hard.

EDMOND: *Yes.*

GLENNA: Sometimes it's hard.

EDMOND: You're goddamn right it's hard. And there's a *reason* why it's hard.

GLENNA: Why?

EDMOND: So that we will stand up. So that we'll be our *selves.* Glenna: *(Pause.)* Glenna: This world is a piece of shit. *(Pause.)* It is a shit house. *(Pause.)* . . . There is NO LAW . . . there is no *history* . . . there is just *now* . . . and if there is a *god* he may love the weak, Glenna. *(Pause.)* But he respects the strong. *(Pause.)* And if you are a *man* you should be feared. *(Pause.)* You should be feared. . . . *(Pause.)*
You just know you command respect.

GLENNA: That's why I love the theater. . . . *(Pause.)*
   Because what you must ask respect for is yourself. . . .

EDMOND: What do you mean?

GLENNA: When you're on stage.

EDMOND: Yes.

GLENNA: For *your* feelings.

EDMOND: Absolutely. Absolutely, yes . . .

GLENNA: And, and, and *not* be someone else.

EDMOND: Why should you? . . .

GLENNA: . . . That's why, and I'm so proud to *be* in this
   profession . . .

EDMOND: . . . I don't blame you . . .

GLENNA: . . . because your aspirations . . .

EDMOND: . . . and I'll bet that you're good at it. . . .

GLENNA: . . . they . . .

EDMOND: . . . They have no bounds.

GLENNA: There's nothing . . .

EDMOND: . . . Yes. I understand. . . .

GLENNA: . . . to *bound* you but your soul.

EDMOND *(pause):* Do something for me.

GLENNA: . . .Uh . . .

EDMOND: *Act* something for me. Would you act something
   for me? . . .

GLENNA: *Now?*

EDMOND: Yes.

GLENNA: Sitting right here? . . .

EDMOND: Yes. *(Pause.)*

GLENNA: Would you really like me to?

EDMOND: You know I would. You see me sitting here, and you know that I would. I'd *love* it.
Just because we both *want* to. I'd *love* you to.
(Pause.)

GLENNA: What would you like me to do?

EDMOND: Whatever you'd like. What plays have you done?

GLENNA: Well, we've only done scenes.

EDMOND: You've only done scenes.

GLENNA: I shouldn't say "only." They contain the kernel of the play.

EDMOND: Uh-huh.

(Pause.)

What *plays* have you done?

GLENNA: In college I played Juliet.

EDMOND: In Shakespeare?

GLENNA: Yes. In Shakespeare. What do you think?

EDMOND: Well, I meant, there's *plays* named Juliet.

GLENNA: There are?

EDMOND: Yes.

GLENNA: I don't think so.

EDMOND: Well, there are.—Don't. Don't. Don't.
Don't be so *limited*. . . . And don't assume I'm dumb
because I wear a suit and tie.

GLENNA: I don't assume that.

EDMOND: Because what we've *done* tonight. Since you met
me, it didn't make a difference then. Forget it.
All I meant, you say you are an *actress*. . . .

GLENNA: I am an actress. . . .

EDMOND: Yes. I say that's what you *say*. So *I* say what *plays*
have you done. That's all.

GLENNA: The work I've done I have done for my peers.

EDMOND: What does that mean?

GLENNA: In class.

EDMOND: In class.

GLENNA: In class or workshop.

EDMOND: Not, not for a paying group.

GLENNA: No, absolutely not.

EDMOND: Then you are not an actress. Face it.
Let's start right. The two of us. I'm not lying to *you*,
don't lie to *me*.
And don't lie to yourself.
Face it. You're a beautiful woman. You have *worlds*
before you. I do, too.
Things to do. Things you can di*scover*.
What I'm saying, start *now*, start *tonight*. With *me*. *Be*
with me. Be what you *are*. . . .

GLENNA: I am what I am.

EDMOND: That's absolutely right. And that's what I loved
when I saw you tonight. What I *loved.*
I use that word. *(Pause.)* I used that word.
I loved a *woman.* Standing there. A working woman.
Who brought life to what she did. Who took a moment
to *joke* with me. That's . . . that's . . . that's . . . god
bless you what you are. Say it: I am a waitress.

(Pause.)

Say it.

GLENNA: What does it mean if I say something?

EDMOND: Say it with me. *(Pause.)*

GLENNA: What?

EDMOND: "I am a waitress."

GLENNA: I think that you better go.

EDMOND: If you want me to go I'll go.
Say it with me. Say what you are. And I'll say what *I*
am.

GLENNA: . . . What *you* are . . .

EDMOND: I've *made* that discovery. Now: I want you to
change your life with me. *Right* now, for what*ever* that
we can be. *I* don't know what that is, *you* don't know.
Speak with me. Right now. Say it.

GLENNA: I don't know what you're talking about.

EDMOND: Oh, by the Lord, yes, you do. Say it with me. *(She takes out a vial of pills.)* What are those?

GLENNA: Pills.

EDMOND: For what? Don't take them.

GLENNA: I have this tendency to get anxious.

EDMOND *(knocks them from her hand):* Don't take them. Go *through* it. Go *through* with me.

GLENNA: You're scaring me.

EDMOND: I am not. I know when I'm scaring you. *Be*lieve me. *(Pause).*

GLENNA: Get out. *(Pause.)*

EDMOND: Glenna. *(Pause.)*

GLENNA: Get out! GET OUT GET OUT! LEAVE ME THE FUCK ALONE!!! WHAT DID I DO, PLEDGE MY LIFE TO YOU? I LET YOU FUCK ME. GO AWAY.

EDMOND: Listen to me: You know what madness is?

GLENNA: I told you go away. *(Goes to phone. Dials.)*

Edmond: I'm lonely, too. I know what it is, too. Believe me. Do you know what madness is?

GLENNA *(into phone):* Susie? . . .

EDMOND: It's self-indulgence.

GLENNA: Suse, can you come over here? . . .

EDMOND: Will you please put that *down?* You know how *rare* this is? . . .

(He knocks the phone out of her hands. GLENNA cowers.)

Glenna: Oh fuck . . .

EDMOND: Don't be ridiculous. I'm *talking* to you.

GLENNA: Don't hurt me. No. No. I can't deal with this.

EDMOND: Don't be ridic . . .

GLENNA: I . . . No. Help! Help.

EDMOND: . . . You're being . . .

GLENNA: . . . HELP!

EDMOND: . . . are you *insane?* What the fuck are you trying to *do,* for godsake?

GLENNA: HELP!

EDMOND: You want to wake the *neighbors?*

GLENNA: WILL SOMEBODY HELP ME? . . .

EDMOND: Shut up shut up!

GLENNA: Will somebody help you are the get *away* from me! You are the *devil.* I know who you are. I know what you want me to do. Get *away* from me I curse *you,* you can't kill me, get away from me I'm *good.*

EDMOND: WILL YOU SHUT THE FUCK UP? You fucking *bitch.*
You're *nuts.* . . .

(He stabs her with the knife.)

Are you *insane?* Are you *insane,* you fucking *idiot?* . . .
You stupid fucking *bitch* . . .
You stupid fucking . . . *now* look what you've done.

(Pause.)

Now look what you've bloody fucking done.

Scene 17

The Mission

EDMOND *is attracted by the speech of a* MISSION PREACHER. *He walks to the front of the mission and listens outside the mission doors.*

PREACHER: "Oh no, not me!" You say, "Oh no, not me. Not *me*, Lord, to whom you hold out your hand. Not *me* to whom you offer your eternal grace. Not *me* who can be saved. . . ."
But *who* but you, I ask you? *Who* but you.
You say you are a grievous sinner? He *knows* that you are. You say he does not know the *depth* of my iniquity. *Believe* me, friends, he does. And still you say, he does not know—you say this in your secret soul—he does not know the terrible depth of my unbelief.
Believe me friends, he knows that too.
To *all* of you who say his grace is not meant to extend to one as black as you I say to WHO but you? To you *alone*. Not to the blessed. You think that Christ died for the blessed? That he died for the heavenly hosts? That did not make him God, my friends, it does not need a God to sacrifice for angels. It required a God to sacrifice for MAN. You hear me? For *you* . . . there is *none* so black but that he died for you. He died *especially*

274

for you. Upon my life. On the graves of my family, and by the surety I have of his Eternal Bliss HE DIED FOR YOU AND YOU ARE SAVED. Praise *God*, my friends. Praise God and testify. Who will come up and testify with me, my friends? *(Pause.)*

*(*WOMAN *from subway walks by. She sees* EDMOND *and stares at him.)*

EDMOND *(speaks up):* I will testify.

PREACHER: *Who* is that?

EDMOND: I will testify.

PREACHER: Sweet *God,* let that man come up here!

*(*EDMOND *starts into the church.)*

WOMAN *(shouts):* That's the man! Someone! Call a policeman! That's the man!

PREACHER: . . . Who will come open up his soul? Alleluia, my friends. *Be* with me.

WOMAN: That's the man. *Stop* him!

*(*EDMOND *stops and turns. He looks wonderingly at the* WOMAN, *then starts inside.)*

POLICEMAN: Just a moment, sir.

EDMOND: I . . . I . . . I . . . I . . . I'm on my way to church.

PREACHER: Sweet *Jesus,* let that man come forth. . . .

WOMAN: That's the man tried to rape me on the train. He had a knife. . . .

EDMOND: . . . There must be some mistake. . . .

WOMAN: He tried to rape me on the train.

EDMOND: . . . There's some mistake, I'm on my way to church. . . .

POLICEMAN: What's the trouble here?

EDMOND: No trouble, I'm on my way into the mission.

WOMAN: This man tried to rape me on the train yesterday.

EDMOND: Obviously this woman's mad.

PREACHER: Will no one come forth?

EDMOND: I . . . I . . . I . . . have to go into the church.

POLICEMAN: Could I see some identification please?

EDMOND: Please, officer, I haven't time. I . . . I . . . it's been a long . . . I don't have my *wallet* on me. My name's Gregory Brock. I live at 428 Twenty-second Street, I own the building. I . . . I have to go inside the church.

POLICEMAN: You want to show me some ID?

EDMOND: I don't have any. I told you.

POLICEMAN: You're going to have to come with me.

EDMOND: I . . . please . . . Yes. In one minute. Not . . . not now, I have to *preach.* . . .

POLICEMAN: Come on.

EDMOND: You're, you're, you're making a . . .

EDMOND: Please. Let me go. And I'll come with you afterward.
I swear that I will. I swear it on my life.

There's been a mistake. I'm an elder in this church.
Come *with* me if you will.
I have to go and speak.

POLICEMAN: Look. *(Conciliatorily, he puts an arm on* EDMOND.
He feels something. He pulls back.) What's that?

EDMOND: It's nothing. *(The* POLICEMAN *pulls out the survival
knife.)* It's a knife. It's there for self-protection.

(The POLICEMAN *throws* EDMOND *to the ground and hand-
cuffs him.)*

Scene 18

The Interrogation

EDMOND *and an* INTERROGATOR *at the police station.*

INTERROGATOR: What was the knife for?

EDMOND: For protection.

INTERROGATOR: From whom?

EDMOND: Everyone.

INTERROGATOR: You know that it's illegal?

EDMOND: No.

INTERROGATOR: It is.

EDMOND *(pause):* I'm sorry.

INTERROGATOR: Speaking to that woman in the way you did is construed as assault.

EDMOND: I never spoke to her.

INTERROGATOR: She identified you as the man who accosted her last evening on the subway.

EDMOND: She is seriously mistaken.

INTERROGATOR: If she presses charges you'll be arraigned for assault.

EDMOND: For *speaking* to her?

INTERROGATOR: You admit that you were speaking to her?

EDMOND *(pause):* I want to ask you something. *(Pause.)*

INTERROGATOR: Alright.

EDMOND: Did you ever kick a dog?

(Pause.)

Well, that's what I did. Man to man. That's what I did. I made a simple, harmless comment to her, she responded like a fucking bitch.

INTERROGATOR: You trying to pick her up?

EDMOND: Why should I try to pick her up?

INTERROGATOR: She was an attractive woman.

EDMOND: She was *not* an attractive woman.

INTERROGATOR: You gay?

EDMOND: What business is that of yours?

INTERROGATOR: Are you?

EDMOND: No.

INTERROGATOR: You married?

EDMOND: Yes. In fact. I was going back to my wife.

INTERROGATOR: You were going back to your wife?

EDMOND: I was going home to her.

INTERROGATOR: You said you were going back to her, what
    did you mean?

EDMOND: I'd left my wife, alright?

INTERROGATOR: You left your wife.

EDMOND: Yes.

INTERROGATOR: Why?

EDMOND: I was *bored.* Didn't that ever happen to *you?*

INTERROGATOR: And why did you lie to the officer?

EDMOND: What officer?

INTERROGATOR: Who picked you up. There's no Gregory
    Brock at the address you gave. You didn't give him
    your right name.

EDMOND: I was embarrassed.

INTERROGATOR: Why?

EDMOND: I didn't have my wallet.

INTERROGATOR: Why?

EDMOND: I'd left it at home.

INTERROGATOR: And why did that embarrass you?

EDMOND: I don't know. I have had no *sleep.* I just want to
    go *home.* I am a *solid* . . . look: My name is Edmond
    Burke, I live at 485 West Seventy-ninth Street. I work
    at Stearns and Harrington. I had a tiff with my wife. I
    went out on the town. I've learned my lesson. *Believe*
    me. I just want to go home. Whatever I've done I'll
    make right. *(Pause.)* Alright? *(Pause.)* Alright? These
    things happen and then they're done. When he *stopped*

me I was going to church. I've been unwell. I'll confess
to you that I've been confused, but, but . . . I've
learned my lesson and I'm ready to go home.

INTERROGATOR: Why did you kill that girl?

EDMOND: What girl?

INTERROGATOR: That girl you killed.

Scene 19

Jail

EDMOND's WIFE *is visiting him. They sit across from each other in silence for a while.*

EDMOND: How's everything?

WIFE: Fine. *(Pause.)*

EDMOND: I'm alright, too.

WIFE: Good. *(Pause.)*

EDMOND: You want to tell me you're *mad* at me or something?

WIFE: Did you kill that girl in her apartment?

EDMOND: Yes, but I want to tell you something.... I didn't mean to. But do you want to hear something *funny?* ... (Now, don't laugh. . . .) I think I'd just had too much coffee. *(Pause.)*
I'll tell you something else: I think there are just too many people in the world. I think that's why we kill each other *(Pause.)* I . . . I . . . I suppose you're mad at me for leaving you. *(Pause.)* I don't suppose you're, uh, inclined (or, nor do I think you should be) to stand by me. I understand that. *(Pause.)* I'm sure that there

are marriages where the wife would. Or the husband if it would go that way. *(Pause.)* But I know ours is not one of that type.
(Pause.) I know that you *wished* at one point it would be. I wished that too.
At one point. *(Pause.)*
I know at certain times we wished we could be . . . closer to each other. I can say that now. I'm sure this is the way you feel when someone near you dies. You never said the things you wanted desperately to say. It would have been so simple to say them. *(Pause.)* But you never did.

WIFE: You got the papers?

EDMOND: Yes.

WIFE: Good.

EDMOND: Oh, yes. I got them.

WIFE: Anything you need?

EDMOND: No. Can't think of a thing.

(The WIFE *stands up, starts gathering her things together.)*

You take care, now!

Scene 20

The New Cell

EDMOND *is put in his new cell. His cellmate is a large, black* PRISONER. EDMOND *sits on his new bunk in silence awhile.*

EDMOND: You know, you know, you know, you know we can't distinguish between *anxiety* and *fear*. Do you know what I mean? I don't mean fear. I mean, I *do* mean "fear," I, I don't mean *anxiety*. (*Pause.*)
We . . . when we *fear* things I think that we *wish* for them. (*Pause.*) Death. Or "burglars." (*Pause.*) Don't you think? We mean we *wish* they would come. Every fear hides a wish. Don't you think?

(*Pause.*)

I always knew that I would end up here. (*Pause.*)
(*To himself:*) Every fear hides a wish.
I think I'm going to like it here.

PRISONER: You do?

EDMOND: Yes, I do. Do you know why? It's simple. That's why I think that I am. You know, I always thought that *white* people should be in prison. I know it's the black race we keep there. But I thought *we* should be there. You know why?

PRISONER: Why?

EDMOND: To be with black people. *(Pause.)* Does that sound too *simple* to you? *(Pause.)*

PRISONER: No.

EDMOND: Because we're *lonely*. *(Pause.)*
But what I *know* . . . *(Pause.)* What I *know* I think that all this *fear*, this fucking *fear* we feel must hide a wish. 'Cause I don't feel it since I'm here. I *don't*. I think the first time in my life. *(Pause.)* In my whole adult life I don't feel fearful since I came in here.
I think we are like birds. I think that humans are like birds. We suspect when there's going to be an *earthquake*. Birds know. They leave three days earlier. Something in their soul responds.

PRISONER: The birds leave when there's going to be an earthquake?

EDMOND: Yes. And I think, in our soul, *we, we* feel, we sense there is going to be . . .

PRISONER: . . . Uh-huh . . .

EDMOND: . . . a catacylsm. But we cannot flee. We're fearful. All the time. Because we can't trust what we know. That ringing. *(Pause.)*
I think we feel. Something tells us, "Get *out* of here." *(Pause.)*
White people feel that. Do you feel that? *(Pause.)* Well. But I don't feel it since I'm here. *(Pause.)* I don't feel

it since I'm here. I think I've settled. So, so, so I must be somewhere safe. Isn't that funny?

PRISONER: No.

EDMOND: You think it's not?

PRISONER: Yes.

EDMOND: Thank you.

PRISONER: Thass alright.

EDMOND: Huh. *(Pause.)*

Prisoner: You want a cigarette?

EDMOND: No, thank you. Not just now.

PRISONER: Thass alright.

EDMOND: Maybe later.

PRISONER: Sure. Now you know what?

EDMOND: What?

PRISONER: I think you should just get on my body.

EDMOND: I, yes. What do you mean?

PRISONER: You should get on my body now.

EDMOND: I don't know what that means.

PRISONER: It means to suck my dick. *(Pause.)* Now don't you want to do that?

EDMOND: No.

PRISONER: Well, you jes' do it anyway.

EDMOND: You're joking.

PRISONER: Not at all.

EDMOND: I don't think I could do that.

PRISONER: Well, you going to try or you going to die.
Les' get this out the way. *(Pause.)*
I'm not going to repeat myself.

EDMOND: I'll scream.

PRISONER: You *scream,* and you offend me. You are going
to die. Look at me now and say I'm foolin'. *(Pause.)*

EDMOND: I . . . I . . . I . . . I . . . I can't, I can't do, I
. . . I . . .

PRISONER: The mother*fuck* you can't. *Right* now, missy.

(The PRISONER *slaps* EDMOND *viciously several times.)*

Right now, Jim. An' you bes' be nice.

Scene 21

The Chaplain

EDMOND *is sitting across from the* PRISON CHAPLAIN.

CHAPLAIN: You don't have to talk.

EDMOND: I don't want to talk. *(Pause.)*

CHAPLAIN: Are you getting accustomed to life here?

EDMOND: Do you know what happened to me?

CHAPLAIN: No. *(Pause.)*

EDMOND: I was sodomized.

CHAPLAIN: Did you report it?

EDMOND: Yes.

CHAPLAIN: What did they say?

EDMOND: "That happens." *(Pause.)*

CHAPLAIN: I'm sorry it happened to you. *(Pause.)*

EDMOND: Thank you.

CHAPLAIN *(pause):* Are you lonely?

EDMOND: Yes. *(Pause.)* Yes. *(Pause.)* I feel so *alone*. . . .

CHAPLAIN: Shhhh . . .

EDMOND: I'm so *empty.* . . .

CHAPLAIN: Maybe you are ready to be *filled.*

EDMOND: That's *bullshit,* that's *bullshit.* That's pious *bullshit.*

CHAPLAIN: Is it?

EDMOND: Yes.

CHAPLAIN: That you are ready to be filled? Is it impossible?

EDMOND: Yes. Yes. I don't know what's impossible.

CHAPLAIN: Nothing is impossible.

EDMOND: Oh. Nothing is impossible. Not to "God," is that what you're saying?

CHAPLAIN: Yes.

EDMOND: Well, then, you're full of *shit.* You understand that. If nothing's impossible to God, then let him let me walk *out* of here and be *free.* Let him cause a new *day.* In a perfect land full of *life.* And *air.* Where people are *kind* to each other, and there's *work* to do. Where we grow up in *love,* and in security we're *wanted. (Pause.)*
Let him do that.
Let him.
Tell him to do that. *(Pause.)* You *ass*hole—if nothing's impossible . . . I think *that* must be *easy.* . . . Not: "Let me *fly,"* or, "If there is a God make him to make the *sun* come out at night." Go on. Please. Please. Please. I'm *begging* you. If you're so smart. Let him do that: Let him do that. *(Pause.)* Please. *(Pause.)* Please. I'm begging you.

CHAPLAIN: Are you sorry that you killed that girl?

(Pause.)

Edmond?

EDMOND: Yes. *(Pause.)*

CHAPLAIN: Are you sorry that you killed that girl?

EDMOND: I'm sorry about everything.

CHAPLAIN: But are you sorry that you killed? *(Pause.)*

EDMOND: Yes. *(Pause.)* Yes, I am. *(Pause.)* Yes.

CHAPLAIN: Why did you kill that girl?

EDMOND: I . . . *(Pause.)* I . . . *(Pause.)* I don't . . . I . . . *I don't . . . (Pause.)* I . . . *(Pause.)* I don't . . . *(Pause.)* I don't . . . *(Pause.)* I don't think . . . *(Pause.)* I . . . *(Pause.)*

(The CHAPLAIN *helps* EDMOND *up and leads him to the door.)*

Scene 22

Alone in the Cell

EDMOND, *alone in his cell, writes:*

EDMOND: Dear Mrs. Brown. You don't remember me. Perhaps you do. Do you remember Eddie Burke who lived on Euclid? Maybe you do. I took Debbie to the prom. I know that she never found me attractive, and I think, perhaps she was coerced in some way to go with me—though I can't think in what way. It also strikes me as I write that maybe she went of her own free will and I found it important to *think* that she went unwillingly. (*Pause.*) I don't think, however, this is true. (*Pause.*) She was a lovely girl. I'm sure if you remember me you will recall how taken I was with her then.

(*A* GUARD *enters* EDMOND's *cell.*)

GUARD: You have a visitor.

EDMOND: Please tell them that I'm ill.

(GUARD exits. EDMOND gets up. Stretches. Goes to the window. Looks out.)

EDMOND *(to himself)*: What a day! *(He goes back to his table. Sits down. Yawns. Picks up the paper.)*

Scene 23

In the Prison Cell

EDMOND *and the* PRISONER *are each lying on their bunks.*

EDMOND: You can't control what you make of your life.

PRISONER: Now, thass for *damn* sure.

EDMOND: There is a destiny that shapes our ends. . . .

PRISONER: . . . Uh-huh . . .

EDMOND: Rough-hew them how we may.

PRISONER: How *e'er* we motherfucking may.

EDMOND: And that's the truth.

PRISONER: You *know* that is the truth.

EDMOND: . . . And people say it's *heredity,* or it's environment . . . but, but I think it's something else.

PRISONER: What you think that it is?

EDMOND: I think it's something *beyond* that.

PRISONER: Uh-huh . . .

EDMOND: *Beyond* those things that we can know. *(Pause.)* I think maybe in dreams we see what it is. *(Pause.)* What do you think? *(Pause.)*

PRISONER: I don't know.

EDMOND: I don't think we *can* know. I think that if we *knew* it, we'd be dead.

PRISONER: We would be *God.*

EDMOND: We would be God. That's absolutely right.

PRISONER: Or, or some *genius.*

EDMOND: No, I don't think even *genius* could know what it is.

PRISONER: No, some great *genius, (pause)* or some *philosopher* . . .

EDMOND: I don't think even a *genius* can see what we are.

PRISONER: You don't . . . *think* that . . . *(Pause.)*

EDMOND: I think that we can't perceive it.

PRISONER: Well, *something's* going on, I'll tell you *that.* I'm saying, *somewhere some* poor sucker knows what's happening.

EDMOND: Do you think?

PRISONER: *Shit* yes. Some whacked-out sucker. Somewhere. In the Ozarks? *(Pause.) Shit* yes. Some guy. *(Pause.)* Some *inbred* sucker, walks around all day . . .

(Pause.)

EDMOND: You think?

PRISONER: Yeah. Maybe not *him* . . . but someone. *(Pause.)*
Some fuck locked up, he's got time for reflection. . . .

(Pause.)

Or some fuckin' . . . *I* don't know, some *kid,* who's just
been *born. (Pause.)*

EDMOND: Some kid that's just been born . . .

PRISONER: Yes. And you know, he's got no precon*cep-
tions* . . .

EDMOND: Yes.

PRISONER: All he's got . . .

EDMOND: . . . That's absolutely right. . . .

PRISONER: *Huh?* . . .

EDMOND: Yes.

PRISONER: Is . . .

EDMOND: Maybe it's *memory.* . . .

PRISONER: That's what I'm *saying.* That it just may *be.* . . .

EDMOND: It could be.

PRISONER: Or . . .

EDMOND: . . . or some . . .

PRISONER: . . . some . . .

EDMOND: . . . *knowledge* . . .

PRISONER: . . . some . . .

EDMOND: . . . some *intuition.* . . .

PRISONER: Yes.

EDMOND: I don't *even* mean "intuition." . . . Something
. . . something . . .

PRISONER: Or some *animal* . . .

EDMOND: Why not? . . .

PRISONER: That all the time we're saying we'll wait for the
men from *space,* maybe they're *here.* . . .

EDMOND: . . . Maybe they are. . . .

PRISONER: . . . Maybe they're *animals.* . . .

EDMOND: Yes.

PRISONER: That were *left* here . . .

EDMOND: *Aeons* ago.

PRISONER: *Long* ago . . .

EDMOND: . . . and have *bred* here . . .

PRISONER: Or maybe *we're* the animals. . . .

EDMOND: . . . Maybe we are. . . .

PRISONER: *You* know, how they, *they* are supreme on
their . . .

EDMOND: . . . Yes.

PRISONER: On their *native* world . . .

EDMOND: But when you put them here.

PRISONER: *We* say they're only *dogs,* or *animals,* and *scorn*
them. . . .

EDMOND: . . . Yes.

PRISONER: We scorn them in our fear. But . . . don't you think? . . .

EDMOND: . . . It very well could be. . . .

PRISONER: But on their native *world* . . .

EDMOND: . . . Uh-huh . . .

PRISONER: . . . they are *supreme.* . . .

EDMOND: I think that's very . . .

PRISONER: And what *we* have done is to disgrace ourselves.

EDMOND: We have.

PRISONER: Because we did not treat them with respeck.

EDMOND *(pause):* Maybe *we* were the animals.

PRISONER: Well, thass what I'm saying.

EDMOND: Maybe they're here to watch over us. Maybe that's why they're here. Or to observe us. Maybe we're here to be punished.

(Pause.)

Do you think there's a Hell?

PRISONER: I don't know. *(Pause.)*

EDMOND: Do you think that we are there?

PRISONER: I don't know, man. *(Pause.)*

EDMOND: Do you think that we go somewhere when we die?

PRISONER: I don't know, man. I *like* to think so.

EDMOND: I would, too.

PRISONER: I sure would like to think so. *(Pause.)*

EDMOND: Perhaps it's Heaven.

PRISONER *(pause):* I don't know.

EDMOND: I don't know either but perhaps it is. *(Pause.)*

PRISONER: I would like to think so.

EDMOND: I would, too. *(Pause.)*
    Good night. *(Pause.)*

PRISONER: Good night.

> *(EDMOND gets up, goes over and exchanges a goodnight kiss with the PRISONER. He then returns to his bed and lies down.)*